IIE RESEARCH REPORT NUMBER SEVEN

foreign student flows

THEIR SIGNIFICANCE FOR AMERICAN
HIGHER EDUCATION
Report on the conference held at the
Spring Hill Center, Wayzata, Minnesota,
April 13-15, 1984

Edited by ELINOR G. BARBER

The Institute gratefully acknowledges special grant support from
the Exxon Education Foundation and the General Service Foundation
that made possible this conference and the book that emerged from it.

INSTITUTE OF INTERNATIONAL EDUCATION
809 UNITED NATIONS PLAZA, NEW YORK, N.Y. 10017

foreign
student
flows

Introduction

The research program of the Institute of International Education (IIE) takes as its mandate the examination, from a variety of perspectives, of international educational exchanges. A brief overview of the current agenda of the program may be useful. In the three years since the program's inception, several studies have been completed: on policymaking in U.S. colleges and universities with regard to foreign students; on the impact of overseas educational experiences on American and foreign master's level students; on the retrospective judgments by returned Brazilian students about their U.S. educational experiences; and on the extent to which and the ways in which American corporations use international expertise in their overseas operations. Other studies, now in progress, have to do with the costs of foreign students to U.S. universities; with the long-term maintenance of professional and intellectual competencies acquired during study in the United States; with the effects of large proportions of foreign graduate students on U.S. engineering programs; and with the process by which foreign students choose U.S. colleges and universities.

By now, IIE has put in place what is, in a real sense, a research program. Such a program has identifiable themes, as well as studies that build cumulatively on each other. The major themes are the following: the relationship between international education and international understanding; the effects of foreign training on the development of poor countries; the meaning of flows of foreign students to institutions of higher education; and the links between study abroad and employment opportunities. As particular studies under this research program are completed, they open up new questions and suggest possible further projects. Initially, the topical focus was on quite general questions of educational and economic impact; "second generation" studies have a somewhat narrower focus, dealing with such matters as the impact of foreign students on particular graduate programs (e.g., programs in engineering) or the effects of interaction between students from particular cultural backgrounds.

In the first completed study, *Absence of Decision* (published by IIE in 1983), Craufurd Goodwin and Michael Nacht dealt with the perceived significance of foreign students for U.S. institutions of higher education. In that study, Goodwin and Nacht interviewed administrators and faculty to find out what they thought about having foreign students on their campuses and how, when it becomes necessary, they go about making decisions about foreign student flows. Goodwin and Nacht found that, by and large, the issue of foreign students has rather low priority for campus policymakers (hence the title of their study) and that, when compelled to think about the issue, policymakers are often at a loss. Certain issues did, however, emerge as salient on the campuses (in Ohio, Florida, and California) that Goodwin and Nacht visited: the contribution of foreign students to the educational quality of the institution, and the economic aspects of admitting foreign students. With regard to educational quality, they found that the educators they interviewed were convinced, without much evidence, that "social and intellectual interaction between the foreign and the U.S. students is an enriching experience," but the educators were also concerned about the extent to which U.S. universities can continue to absorb foreign students, should the number of these students become very much larger. On the economic side, the principal finding was that "educators have a very imperfect notion of the marginal costs to their institutions of foreign students."

The findings of *Absence of Decision* suggested that it would be desirable to deepen the understanding by university and college administrators of the issues presented by foreign students. As they make difficult decisions in the coming years about the quality, scale, and composition of their student bodies and the financial health of their institutions, these administrators often will have to take into account the role of foreign students. IIE, therefore, designed a conference that would enable administrators from different types of institutions to explore further the opportunities and problems that foreign students may create. IIE brought them together to exchange their own views, to consider several relevant papers by social scientists, and to hear from persons with special expertise in the field of international education. This approach is consonant with IIE's more general effort to bring social science to bear on issues of policy and practice in international education. To put this another way, IIE tries to develop interaction between the concerns of policymakers and practitioners on the one hand, and

2

the perspectives and methods of social scientists on the other.

Almost none of the participants in the conference at Spring Hill was a "naive subject;" that is to say, each had, in varying degrees, thought about and dealt with the issues posed by the conference agenda. Insofar as "absence of decision" prevails in American academia, the conference participants were not among those who had somehow escaped or avoided exposure to the issues associated with foreign students. They were aware, at least in a general way, of the various arguments about benefits and costs. Yet no matter how experienced university administrators may be, they tend to see issues and problems from the perspectives of their particular institutions and cannot know in all cases to what extent these perspectives are shared by administrators in other kinds of institutions. Nor is it possible for them to collect and analyze all the many kinds of data that provide the necessary context for their decisions or to identify all the relevant demographic and economic studies.

For the particular agenda of the conference, therefore, two background papers were prepared which examined data on the flows of foreign and domestic students and on the costs that foreign students entail for U.S. colleges and universities. One paper, by Alex Inkeles of the Hoover Institution and his colleague Larry Sirowy, attempts to put the nature and scale of the flows of foreign students to the United States in the context of worldwide patterns of student mobility. The second paper, by Lewis Solmon of the University of California at Los Angeles and his colleague Ruth Beddow, deals with flows of foreign and American students to U.S. colleges and universities, as well as with the average costs of foreign students to different kinds of institutions. Preliminary findings from a third study by Stephen Hoenack and William Weiler of the University of Minnesota, which deals with the marginal costs of foreign students, were also presented at the conference.

Studies such as these are a valuable ingredient in the process of policymaking in academia. They provide needed facts; for example, Inkeles and Sirowy find that the concentration in the United States of foreign students from relatively few countries leaves American institutions and programs vulnerable to policy changes on the part of a handful of student exporters, and Solmon and Beddow report that the same fields of study are generally in high demand by both domestic and foreign students. Also, these studies contain the kinds of interpretations and projections that policymakers should consider in making decisions about the deployment of resources. Yet administrators generally, and academic adminis- trators are no exception, tend to have mixed reactions to social science studies that purport to be relevant to the decisions they have to make. They are, of course, committed to the value of scientific inquiry, yet the results of social science studies may well run counter to common sense, experience, and intuition, and therewith produce a certain degree of resistance. (When results are consonant with common sense they are likely to be dismissed as "obvious.")

A certain degree of resistance may be unavoidable in considering the kinds of projections presented by Inkeles and Sirowy. All apart from the technical difficulties involved in making such projections, it is far from easy to agree on the appropriate assumptions behind them and to accept the legitimacy of the effort to establish long-term trends in spite of its vulnerability to sudden, unpredictable political and economic shifts. However skillfully long-term projections of foreign student flows may be constructed, they are quite unlikely to take into account future events similar to the emergence of OPEC wealth in the early 1970s or to the Iranian revolution at the end of the decade. Yet when all that is granted, sophisticated projections can help avoid the unrealistic expectations and unnecessary concern resulting from the estimate made a few years ago that there would be one million foreign students in the United States by 1990. It is surely desirable that social scientists continue to sharpen their ability to understand the conditions that affect student flows (between countries and within countries) and therewith facilitate effective planning, instead of ill-founded panic or euphoria.

. The economic analyses of costs offered by Solmon and by Hoenack also produce some resistance among academic administrators. While they cannot avoid the necessity of attaching a price to an "invaluable" activity like the improvement of education, administrators find it somewhat difficult to consider general approaches to economic issues in academia instead of focusing on the specific circumstances that enmesh an issue, like the cost of foreign students, in their institutions. In this context, economists are seen as "outsiders" who cannot possibly know what it means to run a particular university in Florida or California or to teach engineering to foreign graduate students. It requires a special effort to accept the fact that these outsiders provide perspectives and data that the insiders, immersed in the problems of their institutions or fields of study, cannot readily have.

One valuable outcome of the Spring Hill conference, then, was the joint engagement of academic policymakers and social scientists with the difficult problems of projecting foreign student flows to the United States and assessing the costs of foreign students to U.S. institutions of higher education. Deeper understanding of both these problems was achieved in the process.

There are some important problems with regard to foreign student policy to which social science has, at the present time, little to contribute, and academic policymakers are on their own in dealing with them. The key issue would appear to be the optimal scope of diversity in the composition of student bodies. Not much is really known by social scientists about the educational benefits, cognitive or attitudinal, of bringing together students of varying national, ethnic, or class origins, yet educators strongly cherish a belief in the benefits of diversity. Indeed, they cherish this belief to a greater extent than do other powerful groups that

4

influence decisions about admission to institutions of higher education. It may be no exaggeration to say that administrators in their capacity as educators would place hardly any limits on the diversity of student bodies. Yet as officials responsible, variously, to communities, legislatures, trustees, or alumni(ae), they realize that the number and proportion of foreign students must remain compatible with other demands on the opportunities and resources offered by their institutions.

A second valuable outcome of the Spring Hill conference was the illumination of the various considerations the administrators of public and private institutions brought to bear on the accommodation of the strongly held value of diversity and other, competing values.

Different readers will surely find different insights here with regard to the issue of foreign students on U.S. campuses—new kinds of analysis, new rationales for certain policies, new glimpses of future patterns. Such insights in themselves justify the conference. Yet more important, perhaps, than particular insights is the process from which they emerged, namely, the intensive examination of the significance of foreign students in the larger context of the objectives of U.S. institutions of higher education.

Elinor G. Barber
Institute of International Education

1.
The Conference Proceedings

Session 1: Sirowy/Inkeles Paper and Discussion

Summary of the Sirowy/Inkeles Paper

As a basis for policy development, there is a need for systematic approach to transnational student flows, based on information about these flows and analysis of the dynamics governing them. This paper reviews the trends and patterns of transnational student mobility worldwide, comparing the scale and composition of flows from different kinds of "sending" countries to the several "host" countries. The emerging trends and patterns are explained in terms of push and pull factors and of "intervening obstacles:" push factors are domestic educational opportunities, national wealth, and linguistic commonalities between sending and host countries; pull factors include quality of education, the availability of scholarships, and political ties; intervening factors, which shape the movement of students regardless of the strength of push and pull factors, are principally government policies of the host and home countries with regard to student movement. Extensive mapping and explanation of student flows permit projections of future flows.

The following facts and patterns are highlighted:

—the number of students participating in transnational exchanges has increased eightfold since 1950;

—the transnational system of student movement is asymmetrical; approximately two-thirds of the world's foreign students are sent by developing countries,

whereas three-fourths of all foreign students enroll in developed countries;
—students from developing countries tend to study the pure and applied sciences, while those from developed countries focus on the core liberal arts disciplines;
—the United States is currently overwhelmingly the primary national destination for students going abroad; only African students went in substantial numbers to a host (France) other than the United States;
—in the last 10 years, West European countries have tended to restrict foreign student flows, while the United States remains relatively open, and the Soviet Union has made efforts to attract more foreign students;
—a relatively small number of countries (15) account for 60 percent of foreign students in the United States, and this degree of concentration leaves many American institutions and programs vulnerable to the impact of policy changes on the part of a handful of student exporters;
—the number of women among foreign students in the United States has been increasing steadily;
—30 percent of all foreign students in the United States are enrolled in only one percent of institutions of higher education; greater institutional dispersion seems likely, considering the absorptive capacity of institutions;
—after 1970, there was a reversal in the proportion of graduate students and undergraduates among foreign students in the United States, with undergraduates coming to predominate; a more balanced state is likely to be reestablished;
—compared to other host countries, the United States plays an especially important role in educating foreign students in engineering, the natural sciences, law, and social sciences.

These are some of the more notable patterns and trends that affect the impact of foreign students on U.S. higher education. They reflect conditions in all parts of the world's educational resources and permit at least cautious projections. The firmest of several projections, each of which is based on different assumptions, indicates that by 1991, there will be 698,000 foreign students in the United States. They will come principally from those Third World countries that experience economic growth in the years ahead. Hong Kong, Korea, Thailand, and Taiwan will be important sending countries; less growth will occur in the numbers sent by most African countries.

Discussion of the Sirowy/Inkeles Paper
The discussion of the Inkeles paper, led off by Michael Nacht of Harvard University, focused on its third part, namely, the researchers' effort to establish ways of projecting future flows of foreign students to the United States. This is clearly a topic of great concern to university and college administrators, one of whose major function is planning. They have heard much in recent years about likely flows of American students to different kinds of institutions and in different

8

fields, though available projections have not been entirely consistent. While all these projections agree about declining pools of high school graduates, and therefore of likely declining flows of students into postsecondary education, the scale or rate of the decline has been forecast more optimistically (e.g., by Carol Francis) and more pessimistically (e.g., by Stephen Dresch). However, projections of foreign student flows have not so far been convincing. University administrators who are aware of them at all know about a projection made in the 1982 publication of the American Council on Education, *Foreign Students and Institutional Policy*, to the effect that the number of foreign students could reach half a million by 1985 and a million by 1990. This projection was based on data from too limited a time frame, without consideration of possible economic fluctuations and political upheavals. In this context, Inkeles' projections make considerable advances, though participants in the conference offered a number of questions and caveats even to these.

These concerns had to do with some of Inkeles' assumptions about the characteristics of the countries that are likely to contribute heavily to the flow of foreign students. A key assumption has to do with the economic characteristics. Inkeles suggested that small and poor countries would not be able to provide adequate tertiary education and would therefore contribute significantly to the flow of students. Michael Nacht argued, however, that the numbers coming from such countries would never be very large and that, indeed, major flows in the past had come from countries with new wealth—Iran, Nigeria, Malaysia, Korea, Mexico, and Venezuela. Joe Neal of the University of Texas at Austin agreed, stating that students come from where surplus dollars are. The fact that the economic center of gravity in the world appears to be shifting to East Asia and that the countries of that region place a heavy premium on education is likely to mean that wealthy countries with large populations will be of far greater significance than small and poor countries. (For example, flows from Asia are already steadily increasing.) Inkeles himself noted that if the People's Republic of China (PRC) became seriously interested in sending students abroad for training, the consequences for institutions of higher education in the United States would be hard to deal with. As he put it, a major move by a mouse (i.e., a small country) makes a big difference only to the mouse, but a major move by an elephant (a large country like the PRC or Iran) makes a big difference to everyone else, including the United States.

Several participants pointed out that it would not be simply the supplying countries, large or small, that would determine the scale of flows to the United States. The nature of the demand here, both for manpower in certain occupations (e.g., engineering) and for students in certain institutions or fields of study, may make as important a difference as economic conditions and university development overseas. Assessment of the demand side in universities is not easy: at the undergraduate level, there are broad, centrally established policies and perspectives, but at the graduate level, admissions policy is made by individual departments and schools. An important factor in determining the demand for foreign graduate students in schools of business and management might be, for instance, the increasing preference of American business for graduates of engineering schools and the corresponding decrease in U.S. applicants; at the same time the supply of foreign students for places in business schools may continue, since the perception overseas of the value of an M.B.A. is likely to lag behind the perception in the United States.

Another factor with an important bearing on the flows of students from one country to another was discussed by the conference participants: the broader economic and political relationships among countries. *Post facto,* the importance of this factor is quite obvious, as in the case of the radical change in the relationship between the United States and Iran. But there was general agreement that the U.S. academic community needs what Inkeles called "alerts" and Michael Nacht called "early warning indicators." Like businesses that have large investments in other countries and carry out political-risk analyses, major "sending" countries constitute important markets for American educational services, and some form of risk analysis concerning likely upward or downward changes in the supply of students would therefore be desirable. Has anyone examined the likely consequences of the reversion of Hong Kong to the PRC? John Eng Wong of Brown University asked. Someone else suggested that the increasing "Hispanicization" of the United States might mean a significant growth of flows from Latin America. Stephen Horn of California State University at Long Beach noted the importance of waves of refugees, and John Eng Wong wondered about the likely impact of the ambiguity of the status of Taiwan. The participants did not mention the current disposition of the U.S. government to improve relationships with certain countries through stepped-up educational exchanges, but that also is pertinent here. Alice Chandler of the State University of New York at New Paltz touched on this matter indirectly by pointing out that it is important to understand the extent to which the major receiving countries do and do not want to encourage foreign student flows, and cited the case of policy changes in the United Kingdom with regard to overseas students.

The participants considered the extent to which the university community plays an essentially passive role with regard to foreign student flows or is able to affect developments. Lewis Solmon thought too much emphasis is being given to the likely interests of the sending countries and that the United States can affect developments. Stephen Horn agreed that universities could not be simply passive, but had to consider the extent to which there are sufficient places in certain fields of study for nonresident students from outside a state (in his case, California) or from outside the country. But representatives from the University of Texas at

Austin observed that foreign students might increasingly exercise choice with regard to universities and countries, and Cassie Pyle of the American Council on Education suggested there might be increasing competition between U.S. and European universities for foreign students. All of this was jumping ahead a bit beyond the immediate questions raised by the Inkeles paper, and the conference participants returned to these issues in subsequent sessions.

Session 2: Solmon/Beddow Paper and Discussion
Summary of the Solmon/Beddow Paper

The overall impact of foreign students on U.S. colleges and universities is small, since foreign students constitute less than three percent of the total student population at this time and realistic projections of future flows suggest that this overall impact will not change very much. It is necessary to disaggregate the relationship between foreign students and U.S. students by different types of institutions and different fields of study in order to understand better what the significance of foreign students may be or, to put it another way, whether this constitutes a "problem."

It is helpful to consider the following facts:

—leaving aside a few outliers, the share of the total student population that is foreign ranges from three to 25 percent;

—according to NCES projections, in the period between 1980 and 1989, the number of undergraduates in U.S. institutions will decline by one million and the number of graduate students by 130,000; this means that in the absence of any additional foreign students, 66,000 fewer faculty will be required, while the presence of more foreign students in the future reduces this effect considerably;

—the foreign student population has grown most rapidly in the field of business and the absolute number of foreign engineering students has also grown rapidly, while the fields of humanities, health, agriculture, and education have shown the smallest relative growth; the fields in which domestic student interest has dropped most dramatically (humanities and education) are in relatively low demand by foreign students, while the fields in greatest demand by foreign students are also in high demand domestically;

—the fields in high demand by both foreign and domestic students are relatively expensive to teach;

—the share of foreign students in undergraduate fields of study has increased very little; overall, the share of foreign students in graduate education has risen only from 11 percent to 16.5 percent, but in the physical sciences foreign students are 23.3 percent of the total and in engineering 42.6 percent of the total; the situation in engineering is unique, but its uniqueness is not recognized

11

and it has caused much furor over foreign students in general;

—foreign students are more inclined to opt for science degrees than are domestic students, and therefore they are getting a more expensive education on the average than the typical American student;

—at the bachelor's degree level, there is no significant concentration of foreign students in institutions with very high or very low per-student spending; at the graduate level, where education is more costly, foreign students seem to concentrate at relatively higher spending institutions, which also tend to be institutions with higher-quality graduate programs;

—at the bachelor's level, in virtually all fields, on average more degrees are awarded to foreign students in institutions where the average subsidy provided to students is positive than are awarded to foreign students overall; at the graduate level, foreign students concentrate in similar institutions, but because of the higher tuition they pay they are less likely to pay less than the cost of their education;

—at all degree levels, the share of foreign degree recipients who pay less than the cost of their education is relatively small: 23.5 percent at the bachelor's level, 18 percent at the master's level, and 20.4 percent at the doctoral level;

—foreign undergraduates are overrepresented at low-selectivity institutions, while graduate students tend to be at medium- to high-selectivity schools; foreigners are graduating with master's and doctorates from high-cost and (generally) high-selectivity public and private institutions that charge tuition (out-of-state tuition, in the case of the public institutions) high enough to cover instructional costs.

Preliminary analysis of foreign students' participation in U.S. higher education would suggest that, at least at the undergraduate level, they are unlikely to compensate for dwindling enrollments by U.S. students, though in some graduate fields, the opposite holds true. While foreign undergraduates are more concerned with out-of-pocket costs and less concerned with quality than are graduate students, neither group constitutes an economic drain on the institutions they attend.

Discussion of the Solomon/Beddes Paper

After Solomon concluded his paper, Larry Litten, who is affiliated with the Consortium for the Financing of Higher Education (COFHE), led the discussion. Litten noted the difficulty of carrying out cost/benefit analyses, given the absence of sophisticated tests. He strongly agreed with Solomon about the necessity of disaggregating the academic enterprise in order to assess the impact of foreign students on various component parts, and he noted that what is good for the system as a whole may not be good for particular institutions, and vice versa. Litten did not think that foreign students were now or would ever be a solution to the enrollment problems of colleges and universities. Nor did he think that modifications in the price of higher education would change the demand for it by foreign students: higher education is similar to mature industries, which increase their market share not by pricing but by improvements in quality. The student body itself is part of the quality involved, and it therefore becomes very important to examine the validity of the humanist presumption concerning the improvement in quality that foreign students bring. To put it another way, Litten asked what the merits of diversity might be for marketing education in different institutions. (It may be important to note that COFHE, the organization with which Litten is associated, is concerned exclusively with the market for elite private education.)

Other conference participants had somewhat different views about the role of foreign students' impact on the enrollment problem. Joe Neal noted that the petroleum engineering program at the University of Texas at Austin has benefited from foreign student enrollments during periods of lesser interest on the part of American students. Stephen Horn, who is also connected with a public university, thought that foreign students make more difference to private than public institutions, although he did not disagree with Joe Neal that in particular fields of study foreign students may be vital.

There was a good deal of discussion of Solmon's way of calculating the cost of foreign students. Alice Chandler suggested that it is necessary to look beyond instructional costs to such fixed costs as tenured faculty; in Europe, where faculties are highly tenured, foreign students can be valuable in maximizing use of institutional capacity. (This argument is related to the one that Stephen Hoenack was to make subsequently.)

In his paper, Solmon argued that only a relatively small number of foreign students were being subsidized, and that of those being subsidized the largest proportion are undergraduates at low-selectivity institutions. When Stephen Horn wondered about the applicability of Solmon's analysis to institutions in his state, California, Solmon countered that the analysis now works better on the national level than at the state level. Michael Nacht reinforced Solmon's point by suggesting that Solmon was working toward a model of an institution that incorporated all the features of public/private, urban/rural, high- and low-selectivity institutions that might eventually be applied to different specific institutions, and David Smock of IIE pointed out that, in principle, Solmon's methodology could work at the state level as well as the national level.

Although university administrators are constantly confronted with economic arguments about their student bodies, they continue to be reluctant to think about these matters primarily in economic terms. Whatever the merits of Solmon's analysis, it will be necessary for university policymakers to examine it in greater detail before being able to deal with it effectively on its own terms. The group at Spring Hill was able to voice certain discomforts with it, some of them surely

13

well taken, but had too little time to assess its applicability to their particular situations.

Session 3: Consideration of Heterogeneity in Admissions Policy

The issue of heterogeneity in student bodies is of central importance when and if decisions are made by universities and colleges about the number and proportion of their foreign students. Is heterogeneity something that in the natural course of events characterizes applicant pools or the student bodies selected from these pools? Should and can heterogeneity be deliberately cultivated? And if so, how do foreign students enter into the picture, and for what reasons?

The discussion was led by Seamus Malin of Harvard University, who expressed a preference for the term "diversity" rather than "heterogeneity." He testified to a "visceral" sense of the importance of diversity, confessing that there was no available quantitative evidence on the subject. In private institutions, he noted, the pool of applicants is, in fact, made diverse by conscious effort, and once the pool is diverse, the process of selection thus yields a mixed student body. For demographic and socioeconomic reasons and because of their historical mission, public institutions come more naturally by the kind of diversity that private ones are trying to emulate.

But life is evidently not quite so simple for public institutions. Steve Altman spoke up for Florida International University (FIU), whose student body comes predominantly (80 percent) from the Miami area, with 10 percent being international students. Florida International has made an implicit decision to try to broaden its mix of students, for example, by increasing the availability of campus housing. There is a sense of the need to "deparochialize" the university and to get it into the U.S. mainstream. Bill Leffland, from the same university, spoke of wanting windows on different parts of the world. As Altman explained, in response to a question from Michael Nacht, FIU is looking to other regions, but not in specific numerical terms; it has its own form of recruiting through networks that emerge in relationships with foreign universities. Altman saw no risk of having too many foreign students, only of FIU's particularly regional risk of being too homogeneously Hispanic.

The University of Texas at Austin, as described by Joe Neal and Bill Paver, exercises control over the foreign student component of its student body. In the undergraduate admissions process, consideration is chiefly given to the academic background of the foreign student applicant, but the applicant's major area of study and country of origin also are considered.

Stephen Horn, the president of California State University at Long Beach, felt that only government-supported scholarships could ensure real economic and geographic diversity in the student body. At the moment, his university gets students primarily from the Middle East and Asia, and the Asians gravitate into science and engineering. The mix of students is largely unplanned; it results from the context in which the university exists (Long Beach is a highly cosmopolitan place, with many different groups of refugees), as well as from a certain amount of intervention.

A very different view was provided by our contingent from Smith College. Few recent immigrants come to Smith, and the college is seeking to create economic and other diversity in its student body. Suburbanites, as Lorna Blake put it, think the same way all over the United States, and since a good deal of recruiting is done by suburbanite alumnae, homogeneity is reinforced. Jill Conway, the president of Smith (not present at the conference), wants the college to be more diverse, and Wendy Winters, the dean of the college, and Peter de Villiers, a faculty member, strongly supported the merit of that aim but cautioned about the great difficulty in achieving it. As Alice Chandler put it, diversity provides enrichment, both in a place like Smith and at her own institution, the College at New Paltz, where American culture predominates.

After a good deal of discussion that generally presumed the merits of diversity and dealt only with the extent of control that different kinds of universities actually have over the composition of their student bodies, John Eng Wong of Brown University shook up the group by questioning the value of diversity and by exploring the question of values underlying efforts to put together a certain kind of student body. He challenged the Florida International University group to explain why they wanted to moderate the influence of local populations on their institution, and why they wanted to admit other kinds of populations. He even suggested that there might be no evidence that foreign students contribute to the internationalization of a campus or that they mitigate the parochial attitudes of U.S. students. In other words, Eng Wong decided to question some unquestioned assumptions about the positive consequences of "diversity" and the motivation for achieving it.

His fellow participants had some difficulty in meeting this challenge. They began at the level of the substance of education. Ted Galambos, who teaches engineering at the University of Minnesota, made it clear that, at the graduate level, foreign students are important to the quality of the student body. Though that may be good for graduate engineering education, it in no way changes the content of this education. Peter de Villiers of Smith qualified this, observing that in some fields, like psychology, in which cultural attitudes are more important than in engineering, foreign students—as well as minority students—do bring new substantive perspectives. But Craufurd Goodwin agreed more or less with Galambos, noting that the trend away from concern with concrete institutions in economics is making foreign students less significant as a source of comparative institutional information. And Charles Sorber, associate dean of engineering at the University of Texas at Austin, reported that foreign graduate students tend to select highly quantitative areas of study, in order to minimize the importance of their language problems. Presumably, these somewhat segregated foreign students are not likely to have much influence on the content of the curriculum. (Sorber also mentioned the historical need to have foreign graduate students work as research assistants in some graduate engineering programs.)

Alice Chandler addressed the meaning of diversity in a somewhat more analytic manner. She spoke of two world cultures. One is the culture of science and technology, with worldwide common values, methodologies, and even language, concerned basically with the advancement of knowledge; it is a universalist culture. The second culture is more particularistic, with components of nationalism and ethnicity, and in this culture the meaning of "internationalism" is not so clear. In the second culture, we appear to be making certain efforts to Americanize foreign students; most of the instructors are Western, whether the students are heterogeneous or diverse. And, by the same token, the foreign students are making some impression on the American ones. But in this second culture, belief in diversity eventually comes up against the limits of our toleration of diversity.

The question of the merits of the diversity that foreign students bring clearly provokes different responses in a country as diverse as the United States than it does in West Germany, which is basically a homogeneous country. Manfred Stassen, director of the German Academic Exchange Service in New York, gave the conference participants some very valuable perspective on this difference. West Germany is obviously making efforts of a quite different order than the United States to create diversity through the admission of foreign students. There are no quotas or other restrictions on the admission of foreign students at West German universities, except in the so-called *numerus clausus* disciplines (medicine, dentistry, veterinary medicine, pharmacy, psychology). But even there, up to 8 percent of all available places for beginners are reserved for foreign students. The approximately 70,000 foreign students in West Germany — a country that has a difficult language, a higher education system entirely different from the Anglo-Saxon or French model, and does not rely on former colonies — constitute ca. 6 percent of all students, a much higher proportion than the 2.3 percent in the United States. Foreign students are charged no tuition and, for approximately 20 percent to one-third of them, there are scholarships available (for travel, maintenance, insurance and books).

The West German rationale for its foreign student policy is much more clearly articulated than that of the United States. Stassen presented three reasons: 1) a belief in the international character of knowledge; 2) an effort to combat provincialism at the faculty and student levels in universities; and 3) a concern to facilitate overseas study by Germans, i.e., to preserve bilaterality in international educational exchanges. For the selection of specific kinds of foreign students for

16

study in West Germany, there are also clearly articulated reasons: 1) the strengthening of the Atlantic alliance; 2) European integration; 3) East/West detente; and 4) a dialogue between North and South. Stassen was quite clear about the fact that the overall priorities in the selection of students do not take into account the needs of particular universities. What is at issue are political concerns, as well as broad issues of science policy and technical assistance. The German Academic Exchange Service, as an organization of the German universities, acts as a broker between these larger political concerns and the more immediate predilections and potentialities of the universities and their funding authorities, the West German States (*Länder*).

The description of West German foreign student policy helped to reveal how different the U.S. situation is, and provided implicit answers to John Eng Wong's questions. However fuzzy the articulation of U.S. policy may be, it is clearly oriented much more directly to the interests of individual students and individual institutions. Geographic diversity, especially at the graduate level, as pointed out by Charles Sorber, is often more of a luxury than a very high priority. If two values — for example, diversity and "getting the job done" — come into conflict, diversity may well get short shrift.

Comments from other conference participants indicated that the U.S. perspective of foreign students is generally a less welcoming one than the German. Stephen Horn noted that foreign students are likely to be lumped together with refugees, and the resentment of refugees by some Americans may spill over onto foreign students. Seamus Malin agreed and added that the "foreign student problem" does not in some cases have much to do with students from abroad but with foreign students from U.S. high schools whose transition to college is often more troubled than their record in U.S. secondary schools would lead one to expect.

Perhaps it is fair to say that diversity is welcomed in U.S. colleges and universities if it opens windows to the wider world but does not permit the breezes to blow too strongly.

Session 4: Economic Aspects of Foreign Students on U.S. Campuses

The economic significance of foreign students for U.S. institutions of higher education must be seen in the context of a variety of pressures on these institutions, Craufurd Goodwin suggested. At one level, there are such major contextual developments as economic fluctuations, the declining flows of U.S. students, changing perceptions of the United States in the rest of the world and the changing role of the United States abroad, international crises that affect foreign student flows, and even a certain cynicism about the value of overseas training for persons from developing countries.

17

How should U.S. institutions respond to these developments? To what extent should they serve their own needs, especially their economic needs? What does the cost of access to education mean for flows of U.S. and foreign students? How do economic pressures affect the desirable mix of U.S. and foreign students? The flow of foreign students from particular regions? Will U.S. colleges and universities compete increasingly for foreign students generally, or only for affluent foreign students? The answers to these questions lie partly in the kind of analysis of the average costs of foreign students provided by Lewis Solmon, and partly in an analysis of their marginal costs, as presented by Stephen Hoenack and William Weiler of the University of Minnesota.

According to Hoenack, average costs are of limited use in institutional decision-making, since they are not related to the incremental resources—instructional time, advising time, space, equipment, and financial aid—necessary to accommodate extra enrollments at the departmental level. Hoenack and his colleagues analyzed the marginal costs of extra enrollments in a number of departments at the University of Minnesota: German, chemistry, agronomy, geography, two departments of biochemistry, and political science. They described these departments, using such characteristics as the respective scale of graduate and undergraduate enrollments (which consume different amounts of faculty time); the quality of the department (and consequent demand for graduate places); the problem of space and equipment constraints; and the size of the department.

Hoenack and his colleagues began their investigation with the assumption that teaching resources were the chief constraint, and this assumption proved to be wrong. What turned out to be more significant ultimately is the time required for advising students. What Hoenack had expected to be "hard" constraints turned out, instead, to be "soft": faculty could often take on new courses; departments adapt and get the teaching job done; class size became more flexible than administrators often thought. The real constraint in taking on more graduate students is time available for advising, and faculty make careful calculations about the advantages of additional advisees. The rewards of such additional advisees vary by field (e.g., it is especially advantageous to have more graduate advisees if they contribute to research) and the most critical consideration in taking on additional advisees is their quality. If the students are good, the benefits of taking them on, including the prestige that is reflected on the adviser, are greater than the costs in expenditure of time. This means, finally, that the marginal cost of foreign students is negative if they are good students; their cost varies with quality, provided they are not in fields that are in high demands.

So much for the analytical model. Participants in the conference looked closely at Hoenack's approach in a number of concrete ways. Stephen Horn and Alex Inkeles wondered why Hoenack and his colleagues had interviewed department chairpersons rather than individual faculty, since presumably it is individual faculty who know best what different teaching and advising loads mean to them. Furthermore, as Inkeles pointed out, faculty styles vary considerably in the extent to which they give time to students. (This is a valid criticism, but Hoenack cannot, at this point, modify his methodology to meet it.) Inkeles also wanted to know what it means, in terms of faculty time costs, to teach the foreign students who actually enroll. As he himself has experienced them, they are often very good, yet still require a lot more time to teach than U.S. students. In short, Inkeles urged that the Hoenack study specify in greater detail the characteristics of the marginal U.S. and foreign students and their resulting costs. Lewis Solmon agreed with Inkeles that the quality of the students affects assumptions. (This is a matter to which Hoenack plans to give more attention.)

There was some discussion also of Hoenack's choice of departments, notably the inclusion of a department with such blatant excess capacity as German and the exclusion of all engineering departments, where, as Charles Sorber pointed out, the cost of equipment is very significant. Ken Tolo of the University of Texas at Austin thought that perhaps insufficient emphasis had been placed by Hoenack on the differences among departments in the proportion of applicants admitted and the ensuing marginal costs. He stressed the special character of high-quality departments. (Hoenack does include one such department, geography; but in his presentation he did not have an opportunity to go deeply into the differences that emerged from the characteristics of departments.)

The presentation and discussion of the Minnesota study provided both useful feedback to the researchers (e.g., an engineering department will be added to the study) and stimulating ideas to the conference participants.

From the consideration of the marginal costs of foreign students, the discussion shifted to other issues that involved, more and less directly, the economic aspects of enrolling foreign students in U.S. colleges and universities. One such issue is competition in foreign students, both among countries and among institutions in this country. Alice Chandler noted the increasing efforts being made in the United Kingdom to attract foreign students; the British Council is doing marketing studies to find out what attracts students to British universities. However, Chandler sees no massive competition for the United States from Britain.

The matter of competition for students has political overtones in some instances, as Jack Reichard of the National Association for Foreign Student Affairs (NAFSA) pointed out. He mentioned the concern in the U.S. Congress about effective competition between the United States and the Soviet Union and the recommendations in the Kissinger Commission's report on Central America that more be done through education to influence young people in that region. Reichard wondered also whether more competition between the United States and Japan for students from Southeast Asia was likely. As the discussion progressed, it became clear that the United States, unlike other countries, does not compete directly as a nation: only U.S. institutions compete. Nevertheless, Cassie Pyle pointed out that this country could do more nationally, if not as much as West Germany, and Craufurd Goodwin agreed, noting that some of the benefits of foreign students—such as development assistance and foreign policy—can be appreciated only at the national level, rather than by institutions. While there is some American national involvement in international educational exchange, as manifested by the Fulbright Program and some of the training programs of the U.S. Agency for International Development, government involvement in the United States is quite limited compared to the national policy of West Germany that Manfred Stassen described, or the policies that have emerged in Britain in recent years.

The implication of this discussion of institutional costs on the one hand, and of competition among countries and institutions on the other, seemed to be that in the United States, a strongly decentralized approach to policymaking with regard to foreign students would continue to prevail. It is the economic impact of foreign students on states, localities, institutions, departments, and even individual faculty members that determines, in large part, the extent to which foreign students are perceived as an asset, not the likely contribution of foreign students to such larger national interests as foreign policy, foreign trade, or the economic stability of the world.

Conclusion

The challenge of the final session of the conference was to capture the significance of the earlier discussions of diversity and costs for particular institutions, and therewith, for institutions more generally. Michael Nacht provided a framework for this session by summing up his own conclusions, and then posing some questions.

Nacht's conclusions were the following:

1) With regard to foreign student flows to U.S. universities and colleges, Nacht foresaw considerable uncertainty about continuing growth in the foreign student population in the United States and uncertainty also about the regions likely to be the principal suppliers. It seems likely that Asia in general and the PRC in particular will be increasingly important regarding numbers of students sent to the United States, but there can be no real confidence in the prediction of trends. The numbers are strongly dependent on political and economic contexts about which it is possible to make assumptions but not predictions. The general view of the group, Nacht thought, was that little could be done actively to determine flows. At least in the short run, U.S. institutions have little choice but to be passive and, at most, to develop ways of anticipating major changes in flows, though given sufficient time to plan, they might tailor programs to appeal to special groups. The difficulty of understanding likely future trends is compounded by the impact

of U.S. immigration policy, another unknown quantity. (Other government policies, aimed at trade and national security issues, come in to play also.) Both external and internal factors, then, are difficult to predict and even to anticipate, but it is worth trying to anticipate them.

2) Although overall flows are hard to calculate, Nacht concluded that the range of U.S. institutions that are now and in the future receiving foreign students seems to be enlarging, and he sensed a likely increase in competition for foreign students. This has to do with the declining number of American high school graduates and the corresponding need to attract foreign students to maintain enrollment levels.

3) The marginal costs of foreign students for high-quality departments, Nacht concluded, are likely to be nontrivial.

4) Nacht illustrated conclusions about recruitment by drawing a curve on a pair of axes, one of which measured the level of aggressiveness of student recruitment and the other the level of prestige of academic institutions. The emerging curve is U-shaped, with high levels of recruitment in institutions of high and low prestige and little recruitment (or at least no admission of recruitment) in moderate-prestige institutions. For these institutions with prestige in the middle range, recruitment is seen as a self-inflicted stigma, an admission of inadequacy. The low- and high-prestige institutions have a strategy; the rest are reactive. Indirectly related to recruiting is the complex set of economic and other relationships being built between certain institutions (like Florida International University) and certain countries; these relationships produce not only flows of students to the institutions but also, of course, flows of teaching and consulting services to the country.

5) In assessing the matter of foreign student selection by institutions, Nacht constructed a four-cell "growth-share matrix," usually applied in the analysis of competitive strategies in industry.

| | | Market Share | |
		High	Low
Growth	High	Star	
	Low	Cow	Dog

In industry, having identified the "stars," "cows," and "dogs," the preferred strategy is to sell the "dogs" and use the revenue from the "cows" to maintain the "stars." Nacht invited the group to consider the applicability of the model to the selection of foreign students, with appropriate translation into non-economic terms. (The "stars" would be foreign students likely to make the most significant intellectual contributions; the "cows" those likely to produce steady if less spectacular intellectual contributions, etc.)

Nacht then gave the participants representing different institutions an "assignment," which was to answer a set of questions: Does the institution have a "magic number" of foreign students? A maximum or minimum? If so, how is it arrived at? To what extent are economic and educational considerations traded off in the admission of foreign students? Is this an issue or not? To what extent does the institution recruit foreign students?

Smith College. Wendy Winters led off with her description of Smith College and its policies. She described Smith as a four-year liberal arts college for women, often thought of as elite. Quotas are not considered at Smith. They have 132 foreign students (out of 2,500) and 75 more from places like Puerto Rico. They do not feel they have a "critical mass" of foreign students nor that foreign students have become a threat. But they have come to realize that it does matter whether the foreign students are European or nonwhite: last year, they had 40 Asian students, including 28 Koreans, and this made the foreign students quite visible. Indeed, the Korean students were seen as a threat by both U.S. blacks and other Asian students. The kind of mix, then, makes a difference.

Peter de Villiers, who teaches psychology at Smith and has been much involved with the college's international activities, picked up from Winters. He noted that the number of foreign applicants had increased for a while and is now stable. The quality of the foreign applicants is better than that of the domestic ones, so the issue of trading off diversity for quality does not arise. Winters elaborated upon this slightly, noting that foreign student and U.S. student grade point averages (GPAs) are the same for the senior class, while in the junior class, foreign student GPAs are higher.

The president of Smith College, Jill Conway, has had an explicit policy of increasing the amount of financial aid for foreign students. In the past, only four scholarships were given to foreign students; now, foreign students compete in the same pool as American students for scholarship aid. Until last year, not as many foreign students were supported as it would have been desirable to admit on quality grounds; this past year, Smith admitted all the appropriately qualified foreign students by providing financial assistance. According to Winters, Smith has been supporting 41 percent of all students and 25 percent of international students, with this latter proportion rising. Most of the foreign students have been coming from the Third World. De Villiers wondered whether, if "too many" foreign students accept the offered scholarships, the current policy will remain tenable.

Lorna Blake, the director of admissions at Smith, said that the college does have a recruiting strategy in Western Europe, but does not recruit as aggressively there as in the United States. Nevertheless, she did not think Nacht's growth-share matrix ridiculous for educators as others might think. Admissions officers do spend a great deal of time chasing the "stars" and perhaps do not appreciate the "cows" for their own good qualities.

Harvard University. Seamus Malin, himself in the admissions office, noted that Harvard consists of at least 12 fiefdoms, all different, and it is impossible to cover all of them. He talked, essentially, about the arts and sciences there.

There is no magic maximum number of foreign students at Harvard, but rather a "natural cap," which results from U.S. applicant pressure. A process of "natural selection" keeps the numbers acceptable, though admissions office staff do have to battle a bit for foreign students. There is, however, a sense of an acceptable minimum (though Malin didn't say what it is). The problem is having to turn away very good students. The paucity of places and the fact that foreign students are not eligible for standard government aid funds creates admissions problems, especially at the graduate level.

Disaggregating Harvard a bit, Malin focused on the undergraduate level. At that level, foreign students tend to become a problem if the university succeeds in attracting a high number of U.S. minority students and financially needy students generally. If these U.S. minority students consume substantial financial resources, foreign students become vulnerable. At the present time, scholarship funds are fairly abundant, but if this condition does not last, it may not be defensible to aid foreign students to the same extent as needy U.S. students.

The visibility of foreign students may become a problem if students make it one, but their choice of concentration is not a major consideration when students are admitted.

The University of Texas at Austin. Kenneth Tolo, associate vice-president for academic affairs, led off the discussion of the Texas situation. A key fact about Texas is that this state does not have a demographic problem; i.e., it has a sufficient pool of students, since applications to the university have increased rather than decreased. Through higher admissions standards, the total number of students has been maintained below 50,000. Simultaneously, an increasing proportion of UT Austin students have come from out of state and overseas.

It is a matter of explicit policy at the University of Texas at Austin to maintain diversity among foreign students. These students constitute about 4 percent of the undergraduate student population and about 6 to 7 percent of the total student population. These are percentages not likely to increase, and there is some pressure to reduce the overall percentage to 5 percent or so.

It is necessary to emphasize that these are university-wide figures. Charles Sorber pointed out that about half of the UT Austin foreign students are in the College of Engineering, where about 12 percent of the undergraduates and 48 percent of the graduate students (fall 1983) were foreign. This was not a problem, he said, while the College of Engineering was growing, but now undergraduate enrollment is being limited, which means that the proportion of foreign students also must be carefully monitored so as not to deny admission to qualified Texas residents. At the graduate level, the expected level is now about 35 percent foreign students. An important factor in admitting fewer foreign graduate students in engineering has been the increasingly high quality of U.S. applicants. The resulting foreign student population at UT Austin is as much due to quality considerations as to political considerations.

Bill Paver, who is in the admissions office, pointed out that the low cost of education at UT Austin also contributes to large numbers of applications from foreign students, who are becoming more sophisticated applicants. He added that foreign student admissions policies are not directed solely at these students but rather apply to nonresident students generally. Chuck Sorber noted parenthetically that there is a "backdoor" route for foreign students to enter UT Austin via Texas junior or community colleges, and that the foreign students who come by this route are generally less strong academically.

University of Southern California. The situation at USC was described by Robert Kaplan, who holds no administrative post at USC and was present as president of NAFSA rather than as an institutional representative. Out of approximately 30,000 students at this private university 3,752 foreign students and 190 exchange scholars (total 3,942) make up the foreign population (14.3 percent). This relatively high percentage has been a matter of conscious choice, based on the notion that only with such a "critical mass" is it possible to have that population capture sufficient attention to elicit the treatment to which it is entitled. Indeed, one administrative officer suggested raising the percentage to 30 percent, but that recommendation was not accepted by the trustees. Kaplan is somewhat concerned that the percentage will not hold, since currently there is much reviewing of the situation and a number of committees at various levels of the university are studying the impact of foreign students. There have been no efforts to set quotas by home country, although it is clear that in the recent past there was an overly large number of students from Iran. Foreign students are actively recruited by USC through alumni, admissions office recruiters, and such organizations as the network established by the American Physical Society. There is a continuing conscious effort to increase the foreign student population, especially from countries which are presently underrepresented at USC.

A special feature of USC is that English language proficiency is not a criterion for admission; foreign students are admitted on their academic record. Such a policy has obvious advantages, but it does tend to make foreign students a visible group in the sense that substantial numbers are enrolled full- or part-time in the American Language Institute. (Foreign students *are* tested for English language proficiency on arrival; approximately half of those tested place at the intermediate or advanced levels, or demonstrate that their proficiency is fully adequate to pursue academic studies.) The faculty of the American Language Institute offers English-for-academic-purposes instruction and provides special instruction for foreign teaching assistants.

As in other institutions, foreign students play a special role in the Engineering School. The 1983 figures show just under 30 percent:

Domestic undergraduates	2,698	Foreign undergraduates	(28.2%)	761
Domestic graduates	1,912	Foreign graduates	(29.4%)	562
Domestic total	4,610	Foreign total	(28.7%)	1,323

The electrical engineering department, rated fifth in the United States, has 36 percent. There is, however, an effort underway to reduce the number of foreign undergraduates, though not of graduates.

USC is an expensive school, and a substantial proportion of foreign graduate students receive some subsidy; there are 81 sponsoring agency accounts at USC covering students from 63 countries and providing subsidy to 22 percent of the students. There is limited financial aid for students who are not either U.S. citizens or California residents; therefore, foreign students must meet high academic standards and must be prepared to pay the expensive tuition as well as the relatively higher cost of living in a large urban area.

California State University at Long Beach. As Stephen Horn described it, California's higher education system has three tiers, somewhat similar to the one in Texas. His own university is required to admit California students who are in the upper third of their high school classes, all applicants who have gone to community colleges, and the top one-sixth of students from out of state or overseas. All of this creates few problems, unless something called "impaction" occurs, i.e., a very high demand by California students for admission to certain fields. When impaction occurs, foreign students are a problem. (This is now the case in engineering, fine arts, nursing, design, and computer science.) In an impacted field, foreign students are limited to 2 to 3 percent. Since foreign students have constituted 10 percent of engineering students, it will be necessary to divert applications from Californian students until the foreign students work their way through the system.

State University of New York at New Paltz. Numbers are not a problem at SUNY/New Paltz, according to Alice Chandler. It is a diversified campus with a wide range of students, 5 percent of whom are foreign. These foreign students provide important enrichment for the campus. Since foreign students are so small a proportion of the total, the issue of the "right mix" does not come up. Also, foreign students are not a problem because the university is blessed with a very good foreign student adviser.

Brown University. There is no magic number of foreign students at Brown.

John Eng Wong explained that to have a "magic number," it would be necessary to have a clear sense of what objective is served by the presence of foreign students and then relate the "right" percentage to that objective or outcome, but there is no such notion of outcome.

There are, in fact, several foreign student policies, which are hard to coordinate. At the graduate level, foreign students are recruited because of enrollment problems: the best students are available overseas. At the graduate level, there are 230 foreign students (or 15 to 20 percent). Foreign student enrollment has probably peaked. The price of admitting so many foreign students is the language problem, so the tradeoff is between high quality and limited language proficiency.

At the undergraduate level, the situation has recently changed. There previously were few foreign students who could afford to come to Brown. More scholarships were offered to them and more came, and now there is active recruitment and a floor or minimum of scholarship aid. This year, the foreign student component in Brown's freshman class was the largest ever, and 25 percent of the foreign students received financial aid, compared to 35 percent of all students. But even with the present floor, the cost of coming to Brown still keeps out good foreign students.

Florida International University. All the public universities in the state of Florida together take 10 percent foreign students, and some of the universities get larger- or smaller-than-average shares. FIU's share, as William Leffland tells it, is a bit larger than average.

The foreign students must prove financial capability, which means, in Miami, having $12,000 a year for expenses, including tuition and books. A limited number of foreign students receive waivers, which are allocated by the various deans at FIU.

FIU does no formal recruiting. There is indirect recruiting, through a network of some 25 agreements with foreign universities, through contacts made by faculty who teach abroad, and through university contracts, such as one with Kuwait which produces 90 students annually for FIU.

Miami-Dade Community College. Very briefly, according to Piedad Robertson, the situation at Miami-Dade is as follows: there is no magic number of foreign students but rather great flexibility; foreign students must demonstrate their ability to finance their stay, but the low cost of fees makes this less of a burden than at other Florida institutions; and recruitment is by word of mouth.

UCLA. Lewis Solmon spoke only for the Graduate School of Education at UCLA, of which he is a dean. This School of Education has been rated the best in the country, but it has the lowest GPAs of any professional school at UCLA and the performance of foreign students has much to do with this. Faculty of the School of Education have great difficulty in evaluating the credentials of foreign students. The foreign students have serious language problems and they all cluster in a few fields, especially comparative education. Solmon is perplexed at this disarray in his school, especially after hearing others at the conference describing the ways in which they seem to have their situations well in hand. He wondered how representative the group assembled at the conference was.

His question was interesting and provocative. The answer seemed to be that those at the conference were, as Stephen Horn put it, "skewed to the international side"; that is, they had unusual concern about the international character of their institutions and had thought through the benefits and problems of having foreign students on their campuses. While most of them no longer were struggling with difficult choices, it was not so long ago, as Peter de Villiers said, that they had done so. And Robert Kaplan added gloomily that at his institution there might be new anguish before very long.

On this happy note, the conference ended.

2.
University-Level Student Exchanges:
The U.S. Role in Global Perspective

LARRY SIROWY
ALEX INKELES
Stanford University

Prepared for the Institute of International Education (IIE)
Conference on Foreign Students on U.S. Campuses,
Wayzata, Minnesota, April 13-15, 1984

Introduction

Today, approximately eight times as many of the world's students are pursuing studies beyond their national borders than were doing so as recently as 1950. Within this overall expansion the United States has fortified its position as the leading country of destination. Since 1950, the number of foreign students attending American institutions of higher education has grown by over tenfold. Today, well over 2,500 institutions in the United States have at least some foreign nationals within their student bodies.

Clearly, this unprecedented rate of transnational student mobility has been facilitated by the conjunction of two major structural changes: the world educational revolution (including near-universal enrollment expansion, the tendency toward the convergence of educational systems, and the diffusion of human capital theories) and global infrastructural improvements (communication, transportation, and funding). Together, these have generated the candidates and opportunity for the growth of study abroad.

Reasons for the attractiveness of the United States as a destination for foreign students are many and obvious (Jenkins, 1983). America's central position in the world community and as a center of intellectual and technological research and development, the great number and variety of potential institutional destinations available here, our *de facto* policy of open doors, and the pattern of decentralized governance and variable standards characteristic of American education have all

31

combined to make America a destination with great pull in transnational student exchange. The American degree is valuable, available, and affordable.

Participation in this global student exchange system is widely considered to be motivated by a host of benefits thought to accrue to the parties involved in the exchange relationship: the student, the receiving institution, the host nation, and the home nation.

For the home countries, especially those newer and poorer, study abroad represents a viable, short-term means by which to surmount the substantial human resource shortages they face in their efforts to achieve economic development and modernization (Fry, 1984; Hunter, 1981; Williams, 1981; Spaulding and Flack, 1976). Moreover, scholars have suggested that study abroad has the following additional benefits for the home nation: it provides a conduit by which new knowledge and technologies can be acquired; it strengthens national institutions; it builds advantageous international economic and political relationships; and it may serve as an avenue to diffuse internal discontent (see Fry, 1984; Hunter, 1981; Goodman, 1981; Spaulding and Flack, 1976).

For the individual undertaking the educational sojourn abroad, transnational mobility enables him to circumvent inadequate facilities, scarce openings, or discriminatory admission policies at home. His stay on the foreign host campus may not only provide him with a personally enriching experience, but, if he returns home (for the sojourn abroad opens the opportunity for immigration), he is likely to find his future mobility chances significantly enhanced (Fry, 1984; Coleman, 1984; Rao, 1979).

To some extent, the major industrialized nations have been considered to have an obligation, owing to their fortunate position in the world community, to open their doors to the world's students, thereby providing a kind of technical assistance (Kaplan, 1983; Williams, 1981; CEIP, 1961). Observers are, however, quick to note that the adoption of the role of host may yield significant advantages. First, to receiving institutions, foreign students represent additional consumers of their product which, as in the American case, helps to buffer these institutions from the vagaries of domestic student demographics (Goodwin and Nacht, 1983). Moreover, foreign students provide a useful infusion of brain power and labor on campus (Rao, 1979; Spaulding and Flack, 1976). Second, American students are commonly considered to gain intellectually and culturally as a byproduct of their exposure to foreign nationals (Eide, 1970; CEIP, 1957). Last, the host nation as a whole is argued to benefit in the long run by improved international relations and goodwill through the familiarization which foreign nationals develop with the host society and culture (Wallace, 1981).

On the other hand, a sizeable number of scholars and officials have come to view the relative explosion of study abroad with growing concern. They feel that a formerly innocuous phenomenon has reached such substantial proportions that it now requires formal attention and critical reevaluation. Hence, consciousness of what Williams (1981) calls "the overseas student question" has risen.

One part of this growing concern focuses upon whether study abroad is indeed furthering the interest and needs of the sending nations, especially when these are developing countries. A number of works reflect this more critical, pessimistic perspective on study abroad. Maliyamkono (1980) and Maliyamkono and Wells (1980) question whether the social benefits thought to accrue to nations through their students going abroad really outweigh the costs. Specifically, they challenge the notion that a program of overseas study has anywhere near the number or degree of positive consequences for the home economy that domestic educational development is seen as having. Tan and Lee (1983) similarly emphasize the underlying implication that it might be wiser, especially for less developed countries, to invest domestically rather than to send students abroad. Others echo these sentiments by arguing that much of what is learned in industrialized host nations by students from developing countries (who constitute the bulk of all those going abroad) may be irrelevant to their home nations' needs. More than that, they argue that the large-scale use of overseas study may result in critical foreign exchange losses, weaken domestic education, foster a native brain drain, and ultimately reproduce technological and cultural dependence (Weiler, 1984; Fry, 1984; Moock, 1984).

A second concern, and the one more integral to this paper, focuses on the consequences for the host institutions and nations. These hosts face a major challenge in discovering how best to balance the obligations of the college or university to an international community, on the one hand, with its need to maintain the institution's health, integrity, and responsiveness to the domestic environment, on the other.

Goodwin and Nacht (1983) ushered in this debate within the American context with their review of our educational policy toward foreign students, aptly entitled *Absence of Decision*. It is important to remember, however, that this debate had already arisen within several West European nations which, as hosts to foreign students, had for some time been confronting relatively larger inflows. The debate in Britain is most widely known, and resulted in a policy of charging foreign students full cost (Blaug, 1984). Such debates, and resultant actions, have occurred in other host countries as well (Smith, et al., 1981).

If the overseas-student question is examined from the host's perspective, one encounters a number of issues. Most major hosts are renewing their assessment of the real costs of admitting foreign students (Winkler, 1983; Blaug, 1981). They ask whether subventions by the host country's taxpayers are balanced or excessive. Moreover, issues such as the effects of foreign students on academic standards (CFSIP, 1982), the equity of admitting foreign students when host nation students go wanting (Williams, 1981), and the challenge of large numbers of foreigners and their distinctive needs to a university's identity and social definition (Weiler, 1984) are issues now raised with greater frequency.

Most critical for many officials of American institutions, however, is the danger that their institutions may become heavily *dependent* on the flow of incoming foreign students. The unexamined policy of extensive admission of foreign students to American educational institutions may pose numerous unforeseen challenges and costs. In particular, the well-known volatility of transnational student flows complicates the decisions educators face with regard to the future health and vitality of their institutions.

As educators in American higher education become more conscious of the roll foreign students play within their institutions, and begin to grapple with issues of the "right" number or mix when adopting far-ranging plans and policies, they will require information about the scale and the kinds of demands foreign students will likely place upon their institutions in the years to come. We here undertake an initial step toward filling the need.

In the first section of this paper, we briefly summarize the patterns and tendencies of change characteristic of the global system of student exchange. In Section Two, we locate the foreign student situation in the United States within that larger context, comparing and contrasting our situation with those found within other major host nations. In addition, we extensively review the patterns of impact foreign students have been having upon various dimensions of American higher education. Throughout, we attempt to present the most current data. In some cases to come, however, the data will be for years much earlier than the current one because certain basic studies were done only for earlier years or the data are not readily available. In these instances we will try to supplement wherever possible, even if only with data from merely illustrative countries.

In the last sections, we shift to the question of what the future is likely to hold for American higher education in terms of the expected number of foreign students and the demands they may make. In this third section, we investigate differential policies toward study abroad and national differences in the pattern of sending students to the United States. In this context we seek to identify the characteristics of countries—educational, economic, social, political—which contribute to the flows of students coming here. Finally, in the last section we review forecasts and descriptions of what may await the United States down the road, and present some of those factors policymakers will need to consider when entering the "foreign student" into their policy equations.

I. Transnational Student Exchange

Seemingly far removed from the concerns of individual educational institutions and the personnel within them stands the worldwide system of educational

TABLE 1

Enrollments of Students Abroad Worldwide and the Proportion
Studying in Four Major Host Countries: Selected Years

Year	Number of Foreign Students Enrolled Worldwide	Percentage of all foreign students enrolled in: (raw numbers are in parentheses)			
		United States	France	West Germany	United Kingdom
1950	107,589	27.7% (29,813)	NA	NA	NA
1955	149,590	24.4% (36,494)	NA	NA	NA
1960	237,503	22.4% (53,107)	NA	NA	NA
1965	349,393	23.7% (82,709)	NA	7.5% (26,225)	4.7% (16,396)
1970	508,811	28.4% (144,708)	NA	5.5% (27,769)	4.8% (24,606)
1975	636,321	28.2% (179,344)	14.7% (93,750)	8.4% (53,560)	7.7% (49,032)
1979	872,677[1]	32.8% (286,343)	12.8% (112,042)	6.6% (52,421)	6.5% (56,774)

1. *Data for the U.S.S.R. unavailable for 1979. It was estimated at 70,000 based upon a 1978 size of 62,942, and an annual rate of increase over the period 1975 to 1978.*

Sources: *Statistics of Students Abroad 1962-68* (Unesco, 1971)
Statistics of Students Abroad 1969-73 (Unesco, 1976)
Statistical Yearbook (Unesco, 1982)

exchange. Nonetheless, any attempt to discern the forces behind, and likely future of, inflows of foreign students to the United States must examine the overall transnational system of student movements. Only by identifying, comparing and contrasting patterns of foreign student enrollment worldwide, and within other major host countries, can we gain a deeper understanding of American higher education's role in that larger system. We thereby improve our capacity to think about the demands foreign students are likely to place on our institutions in the near future. Hence, in this section we briefly summarize the larger patterns and dynamics of world student inflows and outflows.

Worldwide the volume of students going abroad for study has grown by over a magnitude of eight since 1950.[1] As **Table 1** shows, the number of students participating in transnational exchanges worldwide has grown from approximately 110,000 in 1950 to nearly 900,000 in 1979. Today, the total very probably exceeds one million. Since domestic and foreign tertiary enrollments have grown at a more or less equivalent rate, however, the proportion of all those enrolled in higher educational institutions anywhere who are studying outside the borders of their own country has remained rather stable at around 2 percent for the world as a whole (UNESCO 1971; 1976).

To describe and explain the patterns of socialization which these numbers generate, we have organized our presentation around a series of questions to each of which we venture an answer.

A. Where do the world's foreign students enroll?

If we examine this question from a regional perspective, we find that Europe, including the U.S.S.R., has been the primary *region* of destination. In **Table 2** the percentages listed under the columns labeled "enrolled" are estimates of the proportions of the world's foreign students attending institutions within the respective world regions for 1965 and 1973. As shown, over four out of 10 students going abroad enroll in European institutions of higher education. North America, largely the United States, ranks second by attracting approximately three of every 10 foreign students. Following in order, but substantially below these two regions, are Asia, Africa, South America, and Oceania.

Clearly, a central feature of the global system of student exchange is the relatively high level of concentration in the destinations students going abroad select. Around 75 percent have been enrolling in but *two regions*, North America and Europe. Moreover, nearly 60 percent of the world's foreign students have been enrolling in the tertiary institutions of but *four nations* within these regions: the United States, France, West Germany, and the United Kingdom (see **Table 1**).

B. Do those regions which receive the most students likewise send the bulk of the world's students abroad?

The answer is no. As **Table 2** shows, based upon the estimates located under the columns labeled "sent," students from North America and Europe, going elsewhere to pursue their studies, constitute only about 30 percent of the total. Instead, the nations of Asia have been unequivocally the leading exporters of tertiary students. Alone, they account for over 40 percent of the world's total. Furthermore, if we add together all the students going abroad from the nations of Asia, Africa, and South America, we find they represent nearly 70 percent of all the students going abroad worldwide.

Together these figures illustrate another characteristic of the transnational system of student movements; that is, its character as asymmetrical exchange. In other words, many nations and regions do not receive a number of students

TABLE 2

Distribution of Foreign Students Worldwide for Selected Years:
Where They Come From: Percentage Sent by Region
Where They Go: Percentage Enrolled Within Region

(Figures are percentages of world total)

	1965		1973		1979[1]	
	Sent by	Enrolled in	Sent by	Enrolled in	Sent by	Enrolled in
AFRICA	12.5	7.7	14.2	4.8	19.8	NA
NORTH AMERICA	12.6	27.7	12.1	33.2	8.9	NA
SOUTH AMERICA	6.8	4.3	4.2	3.1	5.4	NA
ASIA	41.9	14.6	40.9	13.4	43.3	NA
EUROPE/USSR	21.1	43.4	20.5	43.8	19.3	NA
OCEANIA	.9	2.3	1.2	1.7	.9	NA
TOTAL	**95.8[2]**	**100.0**	**93.1[2]**	**100.0**	**97.6[2]**	**NA**
DEVELOPED COUNTRIES	31.5	75.3	30.2	80.1	27.1	NA
DEVELOPING COUNTRIES	64.3	24.7	62.9	19.9	70.4	NA

1. *Data are unavailable for many countries for 1979 on the number of foreign students enrolled within. Any figures based upon available data would be too misleading.*

2. *Complete information on region of origin is not available. The percentages for which this is unknown are 4.2%, 6.9%, and 2.5% for 1965, 1973, and 1979 respectively.*

Sources: *Statistics of Students Abroad 1962-1968* (Unesco, 1972)
Statistics of Students Abroad 1969-1973 (Unesco, 1976)
Statistical Yearbook (Unesco, 1982)

comparable to that which they send out. For instance, in 1973, Asian nations were responsible for sending out 40.9 percent of all students who went abroad worldwide, while they received only 13.4 percent of the total. Illustrating the reverse pattern, in 1973, students from North American nations accounted for 12.1 percent of all students going abroad, but these same nations received 33.2 percent of the world's foreign students. The disproportions between receiving and sending are, thus, in the ratio of 3:1.

This pattern of asymmetry is further illustrated, and in part rendered more understandable, by the figures presented in the bottommost rows of **Table 2**.

Here we find that the major axis of this asymmetry is level of development. Most foreign students come from developing countries, and yet most enroll in developed countries. Approximately two-thirds of the world's foreign students are sent out by developing countries, whereas about three-fourths of all foreign students enroll in developed countries.

C. What are the main tendencies of student mobility within and across regions?

Table 3 amplifies the points raised thus far, and demonstrates a number of additional global patterns in student movements, by breaking down the inflow-outflow matrix by region.

Three major patterns are apparent in this table. First, focusing upon the highlighted figures on the diagonal, it is clear that *intraregional* student mobility, as opposed to *interregional* mobility, is the dominant pattern within only two regions, namely North America and Europe. Generally, about 70 percent of the students leaving their own European nation to pursue higher education stay within Europe. The corresponding estimate for North America is 60 percent. In contrast, the propensities towards intraregional study by African, South American, and Asian students—largely developing regions—are much lower than in Europe and North America. On average, the proportion going abroad who nevertheless stay in their own region is 25 percent or less.

Second, and paralleling the earlier observation that most foreign students originate in developing countries and yet attend schools in developed countries, **Table 3** indicates that the three great less-developed regions of Africa, Asia, and South America are largely unconnected with each other so far as concerns student interchange. Virtually no students from Africa enroll in South American institutions, and only around 10 percent enroll in Asian institutions. Similarly, few students from South America attend African institutions, and only one percent are destined for Asia.[2]

Finally, **Table 3** goes beyond the earlier observation that Europe and North America are the leading regions of destination, showing in detail what share of the foreign students from various regions of the world are enrolled there. In 1973 North America, meaning mainly the United States, was the primary destination of students from Oceania, South America, and Asia, having drawn 49.8 percent, 49.0 percent, and 34.1 respectively of each sending region's foreign students. Europe, including the U.S.S.R., was the top receiver of students from Africa, having received 60 percent of that region's total in 1973, though it has received large proportions of the students from South America (45.2 percent) and Asia (31.4 percent) as well. The time-series data available suggest that, overall, these patterns have been relatively stable, and probably accurately describe the situation today. However, until more data giving regional breakdowns for years

TABLE 3

Distribution Matrix of World Foreign Student Flows: Selected Years

Distribution of Each Region's Students Abroad Across All Regions

(Figures are proportions)

REGION OF ORIGIN	Year	REGION OF DESTINATION						
		Africa	North America	South America	Asia	Europe/ USSR	Oceania	TOTAL
AFRICA	1962	10.7	16.7	.1	7.3	64.8	.4	100
	1968	16.4	17.0	.1	12.2	53.7	.5	100
	1973	12.9	18.5	0	8.3	60.0	.3	100
NORTH AMERICA	1962	.2	54.6	.9	5.9	38.1	.3	100
	1968	.3	61.2	1.3	8.8	28.0	.4	100
	1973	.3	61.3	.2	5.4	32.3	.5	100
SOUTH AMERICA	1962	.02	30.1	45.4	.6	23.8	.03	100
	1968	.03	41.7	27.8	1.5	28.9	.08	100
	1973	0	49.0	4.1	1.6	45.2	.2	100
ASIA	1962	7.6	32.3	.04	22.8	31.6	5.6	100
	1968	8.1	34.4	.05	29.3	24.5	3.7	100
	1973	5.5	34.1	.01	25.9	31.4	3.1	100
EUROPE/USSR	1962	4.1	15.0	4.8	1.2	74.8	.2	100
	1968	4.5	22.7	6.0	1.6	64.9	.4	100
	1973	1.8	27.0	.6	1.3	68.9	.3	100
OCEANIA	1962	0	38.5	.3	2.5	29.0	29.6	100
	1968	0	49.6	.4	3.8	20.6	25.7	100
	1973	0	49.8	0	5.5	20.5	24.2	100

Sources: *Statistics of Students Abroad 1962-1968* (Unesco, 1972); *Statistics of Students Abroad 1969-1973* (Unesco, 1976)

TABLE 4

Distribution of Foreign Students Worldwide Among Fields of Study:
Selected Years

(Figures are percentages)

Field	1962	1968	1973
Humanities, Education and Fine Arts	28.4	30.3	27.6
Law and Social Sciences	18.5	20.8	22.0
Engineering	19.5	17.8	16.5
Medical Sciences	16.2	12.7	14.6
Natural Sciences	12.5	12.5	10.8
Agriculture	3.3	3.4	2.9
Not Specified	1.6	2.4	5.6
Total	100.0	100.0	100.0

Sources: *Statistics of Students Abroad 1962-1968* (Unesco, 1972)
Statistics of Students Abroad 1969-1973 (Unesco, 1976)

later than 1973 are available, we suggest caution in their use.

D. What do the world's foreign students study?

The fields of study by foreign students for which data are available are the humanities/education/fine arts, law and the social sciences, engineering, the medical sciences, and the natural sciences.[3] They present a complex pattern of activity. The aggregated category of the humanities, education, and the fine arts is the most consistently chosen field. **Table 4** shows that between 1962 and 1973, the proportion studying this category hovered between 25 percent and 30 percent. Close in popularity have been the fields of law and social sciences, and engineering, each with nearly 20 percent, though the former set has usually been somewhat higher. Following are the medical and natural sciences, with averages of 15 percent and 12 percent, respectively. Finally, agriculture, at 3 percent, has consistently been the least pursued field. This should be noted with dismay by all who look to technical training to help less developed countries achieve some degree of self-sufficiency. It suggests very heavily distorted national priorities on the part of the sending countries, and perhaps of the students as well.

1. Do students abroad study different fields from what students at home study, or do they differ according to whether they are from a developing or developed country?

In contrast to what tertiary-level students enrolled domestically tend to study, foreign students, by and large, tend to enroll proportionately more often in engineering and the medical sciences, and less often in the humanities and social sciences (Smith, et al., 1981). Moreover, if we differentiate foreign students by whether they come from a developed or developing country, and then compare the two distributions, we find a most interesting pattern. Generally, students from developing countries tend to concentrate relatively more on the pure and applied sciences, whereas those from developed countries focus on the core liberal-arts disciplines. **Table 5** shows that in 1966, 40.5 percent of foreign students from developed countries, as compared to 23.2 percent of those from developing countries, were studying the humanities, education, or the fine arts. On the other hand, 20.7 percent of the students from developing countries were studying engineering, as compared to 15.5 percent of those from developed countries. These data strongly indicate that a country's level of economic development is an important factor shaping the fields of study selected by its students going abroad.

2. What might account for these two differences?

We note, first, that all but a few societies face shortages of the costly training facilities needed adequately to prepare, in degree and number, sufficient man-power for more highly technical positions. Sending students abroad is an obvious way to compensate for the lack of training facilities locally available. Moreover, less developed countries are even more likely to avail themselves of this means, since the urgency of their need and the severity of their shortages are greater

TABLE 5

Distribution of All Foreign Students Among Fields of Study: 1966

(Figures are percentages)

	Humanities, Education, Fine Arts	Law, Social Sciences	Natural Sciences
Those From Developed Countries[1]	40.5	17.4	10.9
Those From Developing Countries[1]	23.2	21.6	14.2

	Engineering	Medical Sciences	Agriculture
Those From Developed Countries[1]	15.5	11.6	2.1
Those From Developing Countries[1]	20.7	14.4	3.6

1. *The rows do not add to 100 percent due to missing information on fields being studied by some students.*

Source: *Statistics of Students Abroad 1962-1968* (Unesco, 1972)

than elsewhere. Second, where state authorities have greater control over the resources requried for study abroad, as they tend to have in less developed countries, then study abroad will be less linked to personal tastes and more to centrally determined national needs. And it seems likely that national leaders in less developed countries will favor the study of the pure and applied sciences, rather than the humanities. We can hardly offer definitive proof within the confines of this paper, but some of the evidence we present later bears on these issues.

E. How "open" is the transnational system of student exchange?

One last observation on the forces which shape the worldwide system of student exchange deserves to be briefly noted here, although it will be raised again in later sections. It is the tendency to increase formal governmental control over cross-national student exchanges. As with international trade and other global exchange processes, we can assess how "open" or "closed," regulated or unregulated is the international student exchange system, especially as that varies from one region and country to another.

Here we look at the changing national policies of major host countries toward incoming students. Burn (1978), Smith and associates (1981), and the Committee on Foreign Students and Institutional Policy (1982) all agree that since the mid-70s numerous leading host nations, largely West European nations, have introduced much greater control over the number and composition of incoming foreign students, and have acted to formalize admissions standards and procedures. Policy changes in France, the United Kingdom, and West Germany, to name a few, have been cited as specific instances of the growing tendency on the part of hosts to be more conscious of the effects which the more open system had. The governments of these countries now intervene much more actively to shape incoming flows in ways the host government thinks to be more beneficial to the host country. Such changes in the policy of European countries, which recently mainly attempt to limit or reduce their role in the worldwide system of student exchange, have the potential to significantly influence how American higher education fits into the larger global system of student exchange. Against this background, we now turn to examine specifically how transnational student mobility has affected American institutions.

II. The Foreign Student in America

Sixty years ago, in the academic year 1923/24, the number of foreign students studying at American institutions of higher education numbered but around 7,000 (Wheeler, et al., 1925). Over the next 20 years, to World War II, the foreign student population in the United States remained fairly stable and consistently below 10,000 (IIE, 1966).

TABLE 6

Foreign Student Enrollments in the United States: 1954/55 Through 1981/82

Year	Number of Foreign Students	Absolute Annual Change	Number of Institutions Reporting Foreign Students
1954/55	34,232	—	1,629
1955/56	36,494	2,262	1,630
1956/57	40,666	4,172	1,734
1957/58	43,391	2,725	1,801
1958/59	47,245	3,854	1,680
1959/60	48,486	1,241	1,712
1960/61	53,107	4,621	1,666
1961/62	58,086	4,979	1,798
1962/63	64,705	6,619	1,805
1963/64	74,814	10,109	1,805
1964/65	82,045	7,231	1,859
1965/66	82,709	664	1,755
1966/67	100,262	17,553	1,797
1967/68	110,315	10,053	1,827
1968/69	121,362	11,047	1,846
1969/70	134,959	13,597	1,734
1970/71	144,708	9,749	1,748
1971/72	140,126	−4,582	1,650
1972/73	146,097	5,971	1,508
1973/74	151,066	4,969	1,359
1974/75	154,580	3,514	1,760
1975/76	179,344	24,764	2,093
1976/77	203,068	23,724	2,294
1977/78	235,509	32,441	2,475
1978/79	263,938	28,429	2,504
1979/80	286,343	22,405	2,651
1980/81	311,882	25,539	2,734
1981/82	326,299	14,417	2,454

Source: *Open Doors 1981/82* (IIE, 1983)

In sharp contrast, the impact of foreign students on American higher education in more recent decades has greatly increased in scale and reach. **Table 6** shows that since 1955, the foreign student population attending American institutions of higher education increased from around 34,000 to well over 326,000 as of 1982.[4] This means that the rate of growth in the foreign study population has been considerably more rapid than that in the world at large. However, the pace of growth has been irregular in the United States, with some surges; for example, in 1966-70 and 1975-80, alternating with periods of much slower expansion, as between 1971 and 1974.

Nonetheless, so marked has been the overall rate of growth that the foreign student proportion of all those enrolled within American tertiary institutions has moved steadily from being only 1.4 percent in 1955 to 2.6 percent as of 1982 (see **Table 7**). This is not an absolutely large proportion. But its significance is not minor, especially when we realize that the increase came precisely during the period when American citizens were also enrolling with unprecedented frequency. To fully appreciate the magnitude of these numbers we need to recognize that the foreign students enrolled in the United States, if brought together elsewhere, would constitute a student body in higher education larger than the tertiary-level student body found in 115 of the world's countries. Again, in describing and analyzing the foreign student population in the United States, we will follow the procedure of setting forth a series of questions to which we provide such answers as we feel the evidence currently available will support.

TABLE 7

Foreign Student Enrollments as a Percentage
of All Enrolled in the United States: Selected Years

Year	Percentage	Year	Percentage
1954/55	1.4	1976/77	1.8
1959/60	1.4	1977/78	2.1
1964/65	1.5	1978/79	2.3
1969/70	1.7	1979/80	2.4
1974/75	1.5	1980/81	2.6
1975/76	1.6	1981/82	2.6

Source: *Open Doors* (IIE, various years)

A. How does the size of the foreign student population in the United States compare to that in other major host countries?

In 1923, approximately 19 percent (about 7,000) of the world's known foreign students were attending American institutions, giving the United States only a modest leadership role, since France and Germany claimed around 14.5 percent each, and the United Kingdom attracted about 9.5 percent (Wheeler, et al., 1925). By contrast, the United States is currently overwhelmingly the primary *national* destination for students going abroad. In 1979, 32.8 percent of all students abroad (approximately 286,000 students) were enrolled in the United States, whereas France, West Germany, and the United Kingdom attracted, respectively, 12.8 percent (approximately 112,000), 6.0 percent (approximately 52,000), and 6.6 percent (approximately 56,000).

1. How does the size of the student body going abroad from each region which the United States attracts compare to that received by other major host countries?

The United States has been the leading national destination not only in overall terms, but it has also been the single largest recipient, or nearly so, from every

TABLE 8

Percentage Distribution of Foreign Students from Major World Regions Among Leading Host Countries: 1978

(Figures are percentages)

Host Country	REGION OF ORIGIN						
	Africa	Asia	Europe	U.S.S.R.	N. America	S. America	Oceania
United States	21.3	39.6	13.3	11.9	45.0	46.7	51.9
France	34.9	5.5	11.8	5.9	7.5	12.6	2.0
U.S.S.R.	8.6	5.8	11.0	—	7.1	9.4	0.0
United Kingdom	8.1	7.8	4.3	1.3	6.8	4.7	13.2
Germany, Fed. Rep. of	2.6	5.8	13.4	3.1	5.4	4.5	1.8
Percentage accounted for by these five hosts	75.5	64.5	53.8	22.2	71.8	77.9	68.9
Accounted for by all other hosts	24.5	35.5	46.2	77.8	28.2	22.1	31.1
Total of all above	100.0	100.0	100.0	100.0	100.0	100.0	100.0

Source: *Open Doors 1981/82* (IIE, 1983)

TABLE 9

Percentage Distribution of Foreign Students in the United States by Region of Origin: Selected Years

Academic Year	Africa	Europe	Latin America	Middle East	South and East Asia	North America	Oceania	Total
				REGION OF ORIGIN				
1955/56	3.4	15.1	23.2	11.6	31.9	13.8	.9	100
1960/61	5.3	12.6	18.1	13.4	37.6	11.6	1.2	100
1965/66	8.3	12.4	16.9	12.0	36.7	11.9	1.6	100
1970/71	6.0	12.7	20.2	10.3	39.0	8.8	1.4	100
1975/76	14.1	8.1	16.6	18.2	36.0	5.4	1.5	100
1981/82	12.8	8.9	17.0	22.8	32.5	4.7	1.2	100

Source: *Open Doors 1981/82* (IIE, 1983)

world region but Africa. The figures presented in **Table 8** indicate the share of the foreign student population from the nations of each region enrolling in the United States as compared to other major hosts. In 1978, the United States was decidedly the leading national recipient of students from Asia (39.6 percent), North America (45.0 percent), South America (46.7 percent), and Oceania (51.9 percent). Even with regard to Europeans who went abroad, the 13.3 percent who came to the United States to study approximately equaled the 13.4 percent West Germany received. Only African students went in substantially greater numbers to a host other than the United States, even though the United States has been attracting a sizeable and growing share from that continent. Nearly 35 percent of all African students abroad were enrolled in French institutions in 1978, while the United States attracted 21.3 percent.

2. Is the relative presence of foreign students in the United States greater than that in other major host countries?

The answer is no. In spite of the United States' commanding position as a host worldwide, the *relative presence* of foreign students here pales in comparison to that found in the major West European hosts. Whereas foreign student enrollments as a percentage of total enrollments in the United States in 1979 was 2.3 percent, it was 5.5 percent in West Germany, 11.4 percent in the United Kingdom, and 12.8 percent in France (Smith, et al., 1981). It is sobering to realize that for the percentage in the United States to have been comparable to that in France, given the same base number for all American tertiary students, there would have had to be close to 1.7 million foreign students in the United States instead of the 280,000 who were actually there. Thus, while the role of the United States as a host is substantially greater in absolute terms, the relative weight of the foreign student body is much heavier in other major host countries.

B. What is the geographic composition of the foreign student population attending American institutions of higher education?

Table 9 depicts the changing composition of foreign students enrolled here, by region of origin. Several patterns in this table are noteworthy. First, more students come from South and East Asia, representing over 30 percent of the total each year, than from any other region. This continues a tendency long established (Wheeler, et al., 1925). Second, one should note the rising shares accounted for by African and Middle Eastern students, and the falling shares accounted for by European, Latin American, and North American students. Those from the nations of Africa constituted only 3.4 percent of the foreign students enrolled in the United States in 1955/56, but by 1981/82, they represented 12.8 percent of the total. Over the same period the proportion from the Middle East doubled to stand at 22.8 percent.

TABLE 10

Region of Origin of Foreign Students Enrolled Within Leading Host Nations: 1978

(Figures are percentages)

Host	REGION OF ORIGIN						
	Africa	Asia	Europe	N. America	S. America	Oceania	Total #
United States	12.9	55.8[2]	8.2	14.6	7.9	1.6	263,940
France[1]	51.5[2]	18.7	17.6	5.5	5.2	.1	108,286
U.S.S.R.	21.7	34.4[2]	28.4	8.9	6.6	0	62,942
United Kingdom[1]	21.6	48.7[2]	11.7	9.1	3.5	1.8	59,625
West Germany[1]	7.6	39.2	39.3[2]	7.7	3.7	.3	55,337

1. Proportions in the row do not add to 100 percent due to missing information for some students.

2. Figures underlined indicate that the largest single proportion of all foreign students enrolled in the host originate from that region.

Source: *Open Doors 1981/82* (IIE, 1983)

In contrast, the relative contributions of European, Latin American, and North American nations to the foreign student population in the United States have declined. The proportion in the United States who are from Europe fell from 15.1 percent in 1955/56 to 8.9 percent in 1981/82; from Latin America, it was down from 23.2 percent to 17.0 percent; and from North America, it went down from 13.8 percent to 4.7 percent. Nevertheless, Latin America remains third as a region of origin, with Africa now fourth, Europe fifth, and North America and Oceania further behind.

The changes in regional rankings discussed above do not, however, necessarily reflect a true region-wide pattern. Indeed, it is often the case that changes in regional representation result from the waxing and waning of enrollments from a few countries within a region. For example, the rising representation of "Africa" is in good part produced by the tremendous growth of students coming from Nigeria alone, which has come to account for nearly 50 percent of the "African" enrollments in the United States. In addition, the rising representation of the "Middle East" has been heavily influenced by the spectacular flow from Iran, which alone accounted for over 60 percent of the Middle East's students enrolled here in 1980. Obviously one must be cautious in interpreting the more aggregated data based on region rather than country.

1. How does the regional composition of the foreign student population enrolled in the United States compare to that in other major host countries?

Table 10 presents the region of origin distributions for the five leading host nations, including the United States, as of 1978.

Quite evident in this table is the fact that for all the hosts save France, Asia is actually, or is close to being, the largest single region of origin. These figures range from 34.4 percent in the Soviet Union to 55.8 percent in the United States. The African pattern is different from the Asian. In France, where only 18.7 percent had come from Asia, African students made up the majority of those enrolled from abroad. By contrast, African students were not a big factor in the United States. As a proportion of all foreign students they were (51.5 percent) in France, (21.7 percent) in the Soviet Union, and (21.6 percent) in the United Kingdom, but in the United States they were only 12.9 percent of the total. The proportion of all foreign students who are from Europe is also low in the United States. Only 8.2 percent of the foreign students attending American institutions in 1978 were from Europe, whereas the figure was 11.7 percent in the United Kingdom, 17.6 percent in France, 28.4 percent in the Soviet Union, and 39.3 percent in West Germany. Finally, the United States is distinctive in that somewhat higher proportions of its foreign student population have been coming from North America (14.6 percent) and South America (7.9 percent) than is the case with the other major hosts.

C. Which nations are most represented within the foreign student body in the United States?

When we disaggregate, and consider the representation of specific nationalities within American higher education, we observe a number of notable changes over time. The number of countries and territories which sent students here in the past has not much increased. What is unique about the present time is that the total pool of countries which characteristically send a rather large number of students has greatly expanded. Some 20 years ago only a handful of countries were represented by over 1,000 students in the United States; today, over 50 countries are represented by that many of their citizens enrolled in American institutions. **Table 11** lists the top 15 sources of our foreign students in 1960, 1970, and 1982.

Looking at the most recent data, we find Iran at the top, a position it has held since the mid-70s. In 1981/82, Iranians studying in the United States numbered 35,860, or nearly double the number of Taiwanese, who were in second place. Still, the Iranian figure is far below the height it reached in 1979/80, when it stood at over 51,000. Obviously, the dramatic changes inside Iran and the disruption of American-Iranian relations explain this drop, and those same processes promise to have further repercussions. Nevertheless, we must remember that no one country has a truly dominant position as a source of foreign students for the United States. Even at the height of its activity, Iran accounted for but 17.9 percent of all of the foreign students in the United States. Although that was a sizeable proportion indeed, the figure was not a gross deviation from patterns set in the past by other countries. For example, Canadians represented 13.6 percent of the total in 1954/55.

If we shift the focus away from particular members of the top 15 sources, and instead examine the top "sender" group as a whole, then several characteristics are worthy of comment. First, in spite of the fact that a span of 20 years is covered in **Table 11,** membership in these lists of "big senders" has remained remarkably stable. Nine nations have consistently appeared among the top 15. Second, while representing less than 10 percent of the countries sending students to the United States, these 15 leaders have regularly accounted for over 60 percent of the foreign students enrolled here. *This considerable degree of concentration would seem to leave many American institutions and programs rather vulnerable to the impact of policy changes on the part of a relative handful of student exporters.* Finally, year in and year out, the list of the top 15 has been dominated by developing countries. In each period at least 12 of the 15 top "senders" have been developing countries.

1. How do those nations from which the United States receives the most students compare to those from which the other major hosts receive the most?

TABLE 11

The Leading 15 Nations of Origin of Foreign Students in the United States: Absolute Number and Share of Total for Selected Years

Country	Students 1959/60	Percent of Total
Canada	5,679	11.7
Taiwan	4,546	9.4
India	3,772	7.8
South Korea	2,474	5.1
Japan	2,168	4.5
Philippines	1,722	3.6
Mexico	1,356	2.8
Venezuela	1,126	2.3
Greece	1,095	2.3
Thailand	1,006	2.1
United Kingdom	993	2.0
Cuba	935	1.9
Jamaica	902	1.9
Turkey	835	1.7
	1969/70	
Canada	13,318	9.9
Taiwan	12,029	8.9
India	11,327	8.4
Hong Kong	7,202	5.3
Iran	5,175	3.8
Cuba	4,487	3.3
Thailand	4,372	3.2
United Kingdom	4,216	3.1
Japan	4,156	3.1
South Korea	3,991	3.0
Philippines	2,782	2.1
Germany, Fed. Rep. of	2,634	2.0
Mexico	2,501	1.9
Israel	2,288	1.7
Colombia	2,045	1.5
	1981/82	
Iran	35,860	11.0
Taiwan	20,520	6.3
Nigeria	19,560	6.0
Canada	14,950	4.6
Japan	14,020	4.3
Venezuela	13,960	4.3
India	11,250	3.4
Saudia Arabia	10,220	3.1
Malaysia	9,420	2.9
Hong Kong	8,990	2.8
South Korea	8,070	2.5
Mexico	7,890	2.4
Lebanon	6,800	2.1
Thailand	6,730	2.1
Jordan	6,180	1.9

Source: *Open Doors 1981/82* (IIE, 1983)

TABLE 12

Top Five Nationalities of Foreign Students Enrolled
in Four Leading Industrialized Host Countries: 1979

United States	France	United Kingdom	West Germany
Iran	Morocco	Malaysia	Turkey[2]
Taiwan	Algeria	Nigeria[1]	Greece
Nigeria	Tunisia	Iran[1]	Iran[1]
Canada	Iran[1]	Hong Kong[1]	United States
Japan	Lebanon[1]	United States	Indonesia[1]

1. *Students from these countries are enrolled in the United States in comparable numbers or more.*

2. *Primarily due to the residence of migrant workers from Turkey in West Germany.*

Sources: *Open Doors 1979/80* (IIE, 1981)
        Statistical Yearbook (Unesco, 1982)

Adding a comparative note, **Table 12** contains listings of the top five nationalities of foreign students enrolled in France, the United Kingdom, and West Germany. As we would expect on the basis of tables already presented, African nations head the list for France; Asian nations for the United Kingdom; and European nations for West Germany. Clearly, these hosts specialize in the areas from which they draw students. It seems reasonable to suggest that, at least in part, this specialization rests upon former colonial linkages. In the case of France the link is to North Africa, and in the case of the United Kingdom it is to both Asia and Africa. Nonetheless, the lists also reveal a sizeable degree of overlap. For example, Iran is on the list for all four host countries, reflecting its status as a gigantic exporter of students. The degree of overlap would become even more evident if we were to extend the lists to include the top 15 senders. Moreover, one should remember that these lists of the composition of various student bodies are not good guides to the *relative* contribution which various hosts make in taking a share of all foreign students. When we compare the absolute number of students received from the countries listed by each of these European hosts to the absolute number received by the United States, we find that the United States received a comparable number, or more, from at least half of them. This is again a reflection of the large share of all foreign students absorbed by the United States alone.

D. *What impacts have changes in foreign student bodies had on American higher education?*

So far we have concentrated almost exclusively upon describing the volume of international student flows to the United States, overall and from specific regions and nations. This narrow focus engenders the impression that the sole problem posed by foreign students for American higher education is numerical, in other words, presenting more and more individuals to be absorbed. In reality, however, changes in the composition of the foreign student population, and in their distinct preferences and demands for certain kinds of institutions and types of programs, greatly complicate the evaluation of their impact. These factors present American educators with a rather substantial challenge, and one which does not confront institutions in a uniform fashion. To these issues we now briefly turn.

Accompanying the dramatic growth in volume has been a tendency toward the ever-greater diversity of the foreign student population within the United States. We call to attention two kinds of diversity: cultural and sexual.

TABLE 13

Representation of Women Among Tertiary Students
Sent to the United States and at Home:
Average of the National Proportions Worldwide and for Each Region

(Figures are percentages)

Average of women as a proportion of students in:	1970	1974	1979
World			
as % of D.S.	27.8	30.9	34.5
as % of S.S. to US	21.5	24.1	27.1
Africa			
as % of D.S.	16.1	17.6	19.9
as % of S.S. to US	12.5	20.5	20.6
Middle East/N. Africa			
as % of D.S.	24.1	27.9	32.8
as % of S.S. to US	10.8	10.8	13.2
Asia			
as % of D.S.	29.4	30.9	33.9
as % of S.S. to US	21.1	22.7	27.7
Latin America			
as % of D.S.	34.7	38.3	43.5
as % of S.S. to US	26.7	29.4	35.0
Western Europe/Oceania			
as % of D.S.	34.2	39.1	43.1
as % of S.S. to US	28.0	31.2	34.1

D.S.: Domestic Students
S.S. to US: Students sent to the United States

Sources: *Statistical Yearbook* (Unesco, various years)
Open Doors (IIE, various years)
Profiles (IIE, 1981)

U.S. educators now have to assist not only larger numbers of students, but also those from a greater number of diverse cultures. In 1950, 121 countries were represented among the foreign student population enrolled here; today, this number stands in the neighborhood of 180 countries (IIE, 1952; 1982). Moreover, as discussed earlier, more of these countries are sending very significant numbers of students. Hence, it is likely that more institutions are faced with the burdens posed by greater cultural diversity.

Accompanying sheer numerical growth has been the ever-rising representation of women. To illustrate this tendency, we calculate for each nation the proportion of those students coming to the United States who were women. **Table 13** presents the average of these proportions for the world as a whole and for each region of the world. We also calculated for each nation the proportion of those enrolled in tertiary institutions at home who were women. **Table 13** also includes the averages of these proportions so that we may compare the proportion which women represent among students studying "at home" and the proportion which they represent of those who went to the United States from the same "home" territories. The data are given for the years 1970, 1974, and 1979.

We find, worldwide and for every region of origin, that women have been accounting for an increasing share of the foreign students enrolled in the United States, even though it remains true that men substantially outnumber women. The proportion of females sent by the average nation in 1970 was about 22 percent; 10 years later, it had risen to just over 27 percent. This proportion, however, varies substantially across the five regions. Nations in the Middle East on average send the fewest women proportionally, whereas the proportions for Latin America and West European nations are similar and the highest. Regardless of these regional differences, upward movement in the averages of these proportions is evident for each of the regions even though the absolute gains differ. Women are then gradually making inroads into the student population sent to the United States from every area.

1. How are foreign students distributed across American institutions?

Beyond the composition of the foreign student population we can consider how foreign students are distributed across the institutional landscape of American higher education. On the surface it would appear that foreign students are having an ever-widening impact upon American schools. At least, more institutions are being touched, and touched to a greater extent. First, there is the fact that the number of institutions reporting the attendance of any foreign students has grown. Second, the number of U.S. institutions reporting they have a large contingent of 1,000 or more foreign students has climbed dramatically, from two in 1955 to 74 in 1982. Finally, the percentage of all foreign students accounted for by the 20 institutions reporting the most foreign students has declined in a regular fashion since 1970, falling from nearly 30 percent to around 14 percent in 1980 (IIE, 1982). In other words, the foreign students in the United States are less concentrated or more dispersed across American institutions; however, the seemingly profound changes may seem less imposing once placed in context. For example, most of the 3,000-odd tertiary institutions in the United States which have some foreign students nevertheless have very few. In other words, the attendance of foreign students on campuses around the country is quite variable, both in absolute and relative size, and their attendance in large numbers is concentrated among a relatively small number of institutions. Although there are approximately 75 institutions today that have over 1,000 foreign students attending, they still constitute a very small share of all American schools. Another way of understanding this is to realize that 30 percent of all foreign students in the United States are enrolled in only one percent of the higher education institutions.

All in all, some degree of greater institutional dispersion of foreign students would seem inevitable given the great expansion in the sheer number from abroad coming to the United States, and the fact that many institutions already receiving large numbers could not or would not continue to absorb still more. The result was inevitably an ever-widening impact. Still, though widening, the impact of foreign students on the institutional landscape has remained rather selective and concentrated.

Those institutions which received larger numbers of students 20 to 30 years ago are generally still among the leading institutional destinations today. However, the leading receivers of the past have not allowed their foreign student bodies to grow at a pace comparable to the rate at which that population has grown for the nation as a whole. They could not have done so without fundamentally changing their characteristic size and character. This explains why, over the course of the past 20 years, it has been rare for the top institutional destinations to have more than 3,000 foreign students enrolled in any given year.

It appears that we can group the major institutional destinations into three broad sets. The largest consists of predominantly big universities, those with 20,000 plus in total enrollment, with the clear majority under public auspices. This set includes, for example, the University of Minnesota, the University of Michigan, the University of Wisconsin, and the University of California. At this type of institution, foreign students generally have comprised 3 to 8 percent of the total enrollment. The second set of institutions, largely private and smaller in total size than the first, has also been the recipient of large numbers of students from abroad. Indeed, these institutions would appear to be specializing in attracting foreign students, since such students may account for well over 10 percent of the total enrollment in the schools in this set. In this group are U.S.C., M.I.T., Howard University, the University of San Francisco, and the United States International University, clearly a mixed bag except for the criterion of large foreign

55

TABLE 14

Proportion of All Foreign Students in the United States Enrolled
in Private Institutions: Selected Years

Academic Year	Proportion Enrolled in Private Institutions
1975/76	37.9%
1976/77	35.8%
1977/78	37.3%
1978/79	36.4%
1979/80	35.4%
1980/81	35.2%
1981/82	35.0%

Source: *Open Doors 1981/82* (IIE, 1983)

enrollment. Those in the last set of institutions enrolling fairly large foreign student numbers evidently do so in response to local population concentrations and movements which act to define their cachement area. Often schools appear and disappear from the lists of leading receiving institutions, since the circumstances which moved them to the status of being major receivers may change significantly over short spans of time. Among the typical cases of schools in this third set—the local impact institutions—have been Los Angeles City College and Miami-Dade Community College. Although these three sets may be identified, we need to remember that in the final analysis, most tertiary-level educational institutions in the United States receive only a few students from abroad.

2. How are different sectors of higher education affected?

In discussing how various sectors of higher education are differentially affected, we will limit our attention to two distinct types of institutional destinations: public vs. private schools and two-year vs. four-year schools.[6]

a. Are foreign students more likely to attend private or public institutions?

Data on the shares of all foreign students attending public and private institutions have been compiled for but a short time span, only since 1975. Nevertheless, they indicate a remarkable stability. **Table 14** shows that consistently two of every three foreign students arriving in the United States enroll in public institutions. In other words, typically a little over a third of all foreign students enroll in private institutions. The importance of this tendency is magnified by the fact that the proportion for all U.S. students in private schools is a little under 25 percent. These facts illustrate well the point we raised earlier. Foreign students

56

are not just more numbers to be absorbed. Rather, they bring distinct needs and demands which may act to reshape American higher education. To explain these different tendencies, a task we cannot undertake here, one would most certainly have to address how the process of institutional selection differs for native and foreign candidates.[7]

b. Do the foreign students from each region of origin enroll in private schools with the same frequency?

The answer is no. **Table 15** presents the proportions of students who attend private institutions for each region of origin. Students coming from some regions are clearly more likely to enroll in private schools than those from other regions. Specifically, students from North America, Oceania, and Europe are about as likely to enroll in private as public institutions; students from the remaining four regions are substantially less likely to enroll in private schools. Especially noteworthy is the fact that Middle Eastern students appear to be the least likely to enroll in private schools. Consequently, the overall propensity to enroll in private institutions would probably have been significantly higher, except for the substantial inflows from the Middle East during the past decade. And, in the future, if enrollments from the Middle East decline, the pressure on public institutions will be eased.

TABLE 15

Proportion of Foreign Students in the United States Enrolled
in Private Institutions by Region of Origin: Selected Years

Region	1977/78	1981/82
North America	55.9%	54.9%
Oceania	49.8%	42.3%
Europe	48.5%	48.2%
Latin America	35.9%	36.9%
Africa	34.7%	34.0%
South and East Asia	NA	34.3%
Middle East	27.8%	29.7%

Sources: *Open Doors 1981/82* (IIE, 1983)
Open Doors 1979/80 (IIE, 1981)

c. Do foreign students attend two-year institutions?

The story of foreign students' tendencies to attend two-year as opposed to four-year institutions has been more dynamic. As recently as the late 1960s one observer, Clive Grafton (1970), reported that, by far, the majority of community

TABLE 16

Proportion of All Foreign Students in the United States Enrolled
in Two-Year Institutions: Selected Years

Academic Year	Proportion Enrolled
1970/71	10.6%
1975/76	14.4%
1977/78	15.9%
1978/79	16.3%
1979/80	17.4%
1980/81	17.4%
1981/82	15.4%

Source: *Open Doors 1981/82* (IIE, 1983)

and junior colleges remained untouched by incoming foreign students. Only 10 years later, Thomas Diener (1980) stressed the current importance and future promise of two-year institutions as vital to international educational exchange.

Although it remains true that most foreign students attend four-year institutions, the *rate* of enrolling at two-year schools after 1970 accelerated to such a degree that it came to exceed the growth rate for four-year schools. Consequently, the relative proportion of all foreign students who attend two-year institutions has grown apace. As **Table 16** shows, in 1970 this proportion stood at 10.6 percent (or approximately 14,300 students); by 1980 it had risen to 17.4 percent (or approximately 49,800 students). Data for 1981/82, however, indicate a slight reversal, as the proportion lowered to 15.4 percent. Still, it remains substantially above earlier levels. Despite the impressive rate of growth at two-year institutions, foreign students are much less likely to choose such institutions as their destinations than are Americans.

d. How do those foreign students who attend two-year institutions differ from foreign students at large?

Thomas Diener (1978; 1980) has made some interesting observations about the two-year foreign student population. Although a clear majority of about 70 percent of the foreign students who enroll at two-year institutions came directly from their home country, a substantial number transfer after first beginning their educational sojourns at a four-year school, a direction of movement opposite to the one normally expected. Furthermore, foreign students attending two-year schools tend to be different in nationality from the foreign student population as a whole. Specifically, Latin Americans were most numerous, according to Diener's (1978) investigation. That region alone accounted for 40 percent of the foreign students enrolled in American two-year schools. Following in order, with their respective shares, were the Near and Middle East (25 percent), the Far East (18 percent), Africa (11 percent), Europe (2 percent), Oceania (2 percent), and North America (1 percent).[8] Finally, a surprisingly high number of these students are refugees. Diener estimated that in 1976, 38 percent fell in that category. Indeed, Cubans and Vietnamese were among the top nationalities among two-year foreign students even though true educational exchange between each of these countries and the United States was virtually nil. Supporting Diener, although presenting a considerably lower figure, is the work of IIE (1981), which reports that in 1980, 15.4 percent of all two-year foreign students were refugees.

In sum then, it appears that two-year institutions have a special appeal to students from some developing countries, and may very well continue to do so, given both their lower costs and their readiness to offer courses imparting middle- and low-level specialized technical skills. Moreover, the two-year school has great attractiveness to refugees. Since the refugee flow is, however, uncertain as to volume and composition these institutions face a volatile future on this score.

3. How are different types of program affected?

Within institutions of higher education, the impact of foreign students may be further differentiated by examining their distribution across various kinds of programs. In particular, we should ask, what proportions are undergraduate as opposed to graduate students? What proportions pursue degrees in various fields?

a. Are foreign students more likely to be undergraduate or graduate students?

Since 1950, American educators have been confronted by marked changes in the proportions of foreign students seeking to pursue studies at the undergraduate

TABLE 17

Proportions of Foreign Students in the United States by Academic Level: Selected Years

Year	Percent Undergraduate	Percent Graduate
1954/55	61.2	38.8
1959/60	57.1	42.9
1964/65	52.1	47.9
1969/70	51.7	48.3
1975/76	53.5	46.5
1979/80	64.7	35.3
1981/82	64.7	35.3

Source: *Open Doors* (IIE, various years)

level rather than at the graduate level. As **Table 17** shows, in 1982 approximately 35 percent of all foreign students were enrolled at the graduate level. This was down sharply from the situation of but a decade ago, when the proportion in graduate school stood at near 50 percent. Yet, **Table 17** shows that between 1955 and 1970, the growth rate of foreign graduate students clearly surpassed that of undergraduate students. Consequently, the proportion of graduates rose. After 1970, the opposite pattern prevailed, and so the proportion of graduates fell to such an extent that in 1982, the level was below that of 1955. Whether this new pattern will be sustained in the years to come is of obvious importance to university administrators. In our opinion, a more balanced state is likely to be gradually reestablished. We say this because the spurt of undergraduates arriving during the 70s resulted largely from the exceptional numbers sent from newly rich oil nations. In any event, we should not lose track of the fact that any given foreign enrollee is more likely to be a graduate student than is his or her American counterpart.

b. What do foreign students study while in the United States?

What students study while in the United States has likewise undergone some significant changes over time. **Table 18** presents a series of snapshots, commencing in 1955, of how foreign students have been distributed across the major disciplines. Engineering, at around 22 to 23 percent, has consistently been studied by more foreign students than any other field. Similarly consistent, but telling a sadder tale, are the figures for agriculture, which are among the lowest in each distribution.

But beyond these two stable extremes, a good deal of movement has occurred. Foremost among the changes has been the rising popularity of the programs in business and management and in mathematics and the computer sciences. In contrast, one may note the declining popularity of the humanities, the social sciences, and the health professions. Receiving only an estimated 8.6 percent of all foreign students in 1955, business and management programs rose to second rank by 1982, when they attracted 18.2 percent of the total. Nearly as impressive has been the rise of mathematics and the computer sciences, from a mere 1.3 percent in 1955 to a 6.9 percent share in 1982. Consequently, these programs rose from the last tenth place to the middle fifth place. In contrast, the proportion studying the humanities fell from 16.1 percent in 1955, when it ranked second, to only 3.9 percent in 1982. The social sciences, although they have remained among the top four areas of study, received about half the proportion of foreign students in 1982 as they did in 1955. Finally, it is worth noting that the proportion of foreign students pursuing further education in the health professions in the United States has also fallen, down from 9.3 percent in 1955 to just 3.6 percent in 1982.

TABLE 18

Rankings of Fields of Study Shares for Foreign Students in the United States: Selected Years

1954/55		Percent in
1.	Engineering	22.3
2.	Humanities	16.1
3.	Social Sciences	14.7
4.	Natural and Life Sciences	10.7
5.	Health Professions	9.3
6.	Business/Management	8.6
7.	Fine and Applied Arts	5.8
8.	Education	4.3
9.	Agriculture	3.5
10.	Math and Computer Sciences	1.3
	Other	3.4
		100.0

1964/65		Percent in
1.	Engineering	22.0
2.	Social Sciences	15.4
3.	Humanities	14.8
4.	Natural and Life Sciences	14.3
5.	Business/Management	8.7
6.	Health Professions	6.0
7.	Education	4.9
8.	Fine and Applied Arts	4.8
9.	Agriculture	3.9
10.	Math and Computer Sciences	3.3
	Other	1.9
		100.0

1975/76		Percent in
1.	Engineering	23.4
2.	Business/Management	16.0
3.	Natural and Life Sciences	13.3
4.	Social Sciences	11.6
5.	Humanities	8.4
6.	Education	5.5
7.	Math and Computer Sciences	5.1
8.	Fine and Applied Arts	4.6
9.	Health Professions	4.0
10.	Agriculture	2.9
	Other	5.2
		100.0

1981/82[1]		Percent in
1.	Engineering	23.1
2.	Business/Management	18.2
3.	Social Sciences	7.7
4.	Natural and Life Sciences	7.6
5.	Math and Computer Sciences	6.9
6.	Fine and Applied Arts	4.7
7.	Humanities	3.9
8.	Education	3.8
9.	Health Professions	3.6
10.	Agriculture	2.7
	Other	17.8
		100.0

1. *Adoption of a new system to classify students (IIE, 1983)*

Source: *Open Doors* (IIE, various years)

All in all, these aggregated distributions tend to oversimplify reality. Departments in American institutions appear to be fulfilling slightly different roles for students from different regions. This is seen most clearly when we examine the proportion of students from each region who pursue studies in, for example, engineering or the humanities. In each case, the regional variation is substantial. For example, in 1975/76, 30 percent of the students from Asia were studying engineering, but only 13.3 percent of the students from Europe were doing so. In the same year, only 5.6 percent of the students from Africa were studying the humanities, while 14.5 percent of the students from Europe were doing so (IIE, 1978). Since what is studied is clearly sensitive to the regional composition of the incoming foreign student population, and since the regional composition can shift without producing any changes in the absolute number of incoming students, educators will need to consider more than the mere growth or decline in numbers when making their plans and policies.

c. Do foreign students pursue studies in the same fields when they study in countries other than the United States?

The answer to this question may hold important implications for the future demands which foreign students will make on U.S. institutions should other major hosts place even more restrictions on the foreign student's access to certain fields. The figures in **Table 19** show how the proportions of foreign students studying various categories of disciplines in the United States during the year 1973/74 compare to the proportions for foreign students studying those disciplines else-

TABLE 19

Distribution by Field of Study for Students Studying Away from Home in the United States Versus All Other Hosts: 1973/74

(Figures are percentages)

Field of Study	United States	Rest of the World
Humanities, Education and the Fine Arts	24.4	31.0
Law and Social Sciences	27.0	21.9
Natural Sciences	15.0	10.1
Engineering	23.8	15.1
Medical Sciences	6.6	18.8
Agriculture	2.8	3.2
Total number for which field of study known:	130,984	348,932

Sources: *Statistics of Students Abroad 1969-1973* (Unesco, 1976)
Open Doors 1973/74 (IIE, 1975)

where. Please note that these categories do not perfectly correspond to those just presented for the United States alone.

This table indicates that foreign students coming to the United States are more likely to pursue studies in the natural sciences, in engineering, or in the law and social sciences than are their counterparts elsewhere. Correspondingly, those who enroll in the United States are *less* likely to study the humanities, education, and the fine arts, and much less likely to study the medical sciences. Hence, American higher education appears to be fulfilling a somewhat distinct role for the world's students going abroad.

TABLE 20
Estimates of the Share of the World's Foreign Students Enrolled
in the United States by Field of Study: 1973/74

(Figures are percentages)

Field of Study	Share in the United States
All fields	27.3[1]
Humanities, Education and the Fine Arts	22.8
Law and Social Sciences	31.7
Natural Sciences	35.8
Engineering	37.2
Medical Sciences	11.6
Agriculture	25.0

1. *This figure is based upon only those foreign students for which the field of study was known in 1973/ 74: 479,396 foreign students worldwide and 130,984 foreign students in the United States.*

Sources: *Statistics of Students Abroad 1969-1973* (Unesco, 1976)
     Open Doors 1973/74 (IIE, 1975)

The data shown in **Table 20** further amplify this point. The figures presented in this table are estimates of the proportion of the world's foreign students studying each set of disciplines who are stuyding them in the United States. For example, 37.2 percent of all foreign students studying engineering are studying it in American institutions. To interpret these figures, we should compare this and comparable figures with the proportion of all foreign students enrolled in the United States, which stood at 27.3 percent in the year 1973/74. The latter figure is, in essence, the expected value for the proportions in **Table 20**. Using that expected value, we can judge how important American higher education is for training students from abroad in the different disciplines. The figures in **Table 20** suggest that the United States plays an especially significant role in educating foreign students in engineering, the natural sciences, and the law and social sciences, and carries a lower burden in the medical sciences and humanities.

d. How important are foreign students to the graduate departments of American institutions?

The distinct role played by the United States in training for certain fields is especially evident in the enrollment pattern of foreign students within the uppermost level of higher education.[9] Toward this end we present in **Table 21,** for several different academic years, the share of doctorates conferred upon foreign nationals.

The top row in **Table 21** shows that in the neighborhood of 15 percent of all doctorates awarded in the United States over the past 10 years have been conferred upon foreign nationals. This figure is rendered even more impressive when we recall that foreign nationals constitute less than 3 percent of the American student body. This contributes to the fact that the vitality and health of many graduate departments are intimately linked to the flow of incoming foreign students. In no area is this point more evident than in the field of engineering. As **Table 21** shows, foreign nationals have been earning such a steadily rising share of the doctorates awarded in engineering that today around half are earned by them. Though the shares for the remaining fields are considerably below this level, most remain sizeable and promise to remain so. We say this because we expect the demand for graduate training to persist for many years to come, regardless of what happens to foreign undergraduate enrollments.

TABLE 21

Percentage of Those Receiving Doctor's Degrees in the United States Who Are Foreign Citizens by Field of Study: Selected Years

	1973/74	**1975/76**	**1979/80**
All Fields	16.1	15.2	15.9
1. Engineering	40.1	42.4	46.3
2. Math	24.8	23.7	27.1
3. Physical Sciences	22.6	22.2	21.6
4. Life Sciences	21.9	18.7	17.6
5. Professional Fields[1]	14.1	15.3	15.4
6. Social Sciences	12.4	12.0	11.6
7. Humanities	8.7	8.6	8.8
8. Education	5.7	5.9	8.2

1. *Professional Fields includes theology, business administration, home economics, journalism, speech and hearing studies, law, social work, and library science.*

Source: *Digest of Education Statistics* (1981)

III. Explaining Transnational Student Mobility

We have, so far, paid little attention to the processes generating the flows of foreign students which we have described. In this section, therefore, we try to go beyond the mere extrapolation of recent trends and seek to further our understanding of the social forces which govern the mobility of foreign students.[10] We can here make only the most modest start on this task, whose future completion is a necessary condition for really sound policy decisions resting on a thorough understanding of the dynamic forces shaping the flow of foreign students and their needs and demands.

The flow of students from a nation can be approached in a similar manner to the way we approach the movements of people for any purpose, that is, by a push-pull model (Lee, 1966). In such a model the flow of students going abroad is a function of the combined "pull" factors and "push" factors as influenced by intervening obstacles. In other words, the transnational mobility of students is affected by factors which hold or repel on the home side, factors which attract or repel on the host side or destination, and factors intervening which facilitate or inhibit the sojourns.

A. Push Factors

Push factors include obstacles to admission to native universities created by limited openings or by social discrimination; lack of training facilities in the subjects which native students wish to study; the perceived or actual poor quality of the instruction which is actually offered; and the hope that foreign training will better equip one in competition for prestigious positions or for successful emigration.

B. Pull Factors

When, in the introduction, we spoke of the general attractiveness of American higher education we were in essence discussing *pull* factors characterizing the United States as a potential destination. Pull factors serve as incentives for the selection of any country as the place to undergo training. Included among these are cultural and linguistic similarity, the availability of scholarships, the fit between the potential host's educational system and system of the home nation, political ties, and the direct cost of schooling. Of these, cultural and linguistic similarities are likely to be most enduring. Political ties, schooling costs, and educational policies are perhaps the most apt to change over time. When these change for some potential hosts, and not others, they are likely to result, in the long run, in the redirection of flows within the transnational system.

C. Intervening Obstacles

Intervening obstacles are those factors which are assumed to constrain and shape movement regardless of the strength of the push and pull factors. Most often we think of distance as the central obstacle. In recent times, however, large-scale student mobility has been facilitated by the diminution of the importance of distance. Infrastructural improvements in communication and transportation have made the obstacle of distance more readily surmountable. Moreover, the importance of distance as an obstacle tends to diminish as the flows between a specific host and home country become more extensive and longer lasting, because with time the exchange becomes institutionalized and even routinized.

1. Intervening Obstacles Created by Governments

Another sort of intervening obstacle is the common governmentally promulgated restriction or even prohibition on transnational student mobility. These may be created by actions of the government on both the host and home side.

a. By Host Governments

The major host countries differ in the degree to which they regulate and restrict the entrance of foreign students into their systems of higher education (Hall, 1971). At one end of the continuum we find a very formal arrangement, exemplified by France, where bilateral or multilateral agreements concluded with other countries precisely define the equivalence and validity of the degrees necessary for entrance. At the opposite end, well exemplified by the United States, are the rather informal and pragmatic arrangements marked by decentralization and lack of strict standardization. This approach more or less creates a de facto national policy of open doors. Somewhere in the middle we might locate a host such as the United Kingdom.

Within this framework, however, changes have been widely occurring (Burn, 1978; Smith, et al., 1981; CFSIP, 1982). Generally, these changes involve the introduction of ever greater regulation by governments of the incoming student flows, but the consequences for the students who would come from abroad have not been uniform.

Smith and associates (1981) classify these regulatory measures, which have been introduced by a number of host countries throughout the 70s, into two types. Some measures tighten admission requirements which may be linked to a numerus clausus. Others abolish tuition fee differentials, which may have favored the foreign student, or follow the path of raising of tuition fees in general. Such means have been used in Canada, Great Britain, Ireland, and Belgium (Smith, et al., 1981).

One example of the regulation of numbers is a quota system, often applied to only a few fields or to a few schools within the host country. Such measures are now in place in West Germany, Denmark, Spain, and the Netherlands (Burn, 1978; Smith, et al., 1981). A second variety regulates numbers by facing the foreign student with generally stiffer admission standards. This approach has been adopted in Italy. In France, the admission procedure has been further controlled by taking away from the individual institution its traditional authority to admit and transferring it to a central commission. Moreover, admission standards have been tightened by requiring prospective students to pass a French language examination while still in their home country, and to prove they have sufficient funds for the duration of their studies.

As Smith and associates (1981) note, these policies do not pose an equally imposing obstacle to all foreign students alike. Instead, they are designed to shape differentially the incoming flow of students through built-in exceptions and preferences. By and large, these policies favor the continued flow of students from developing countries, students who will enroll in graduate programs, those who will enroll for short-term training, and those who would like to pursue studies in certain fields such as the medical sciences. Of course legislated preferences favoring some imply formidable barriers to others.

The Soviet Union, in contradistinction to other European hosts, has actively encouraged the inward flow of foreign students in recent years (CFSIP, 1982). Nearly universally supported by Soviet state scholarships, massive numbers of students from non-communist developing nations have been entering the U.S.S.R. over recent years. These encouraged inflows are clear expressions of official state policies.

In contrast to other hosts, the United States is distinctive in its lack of centralized and standard national means to regulate foreign student inflows. The United States officially seems neither to favor or disfavor the flows in general terms, even though it may discriminate in the particular sources. The Committee on Foreign Students and Institutional Policy (1982) observed that the U.S. federal government seems to have less an official policy toward foreign students than an informal view of the worth of maintaining an open doors policy. A policy of noninterference and ideological support by government has been espoused on the grounds that it is in America's national and international interests. Support for such a policy also comes in the form of the argument that the exchange benefits developing nations. These and other considerations involved in the U.S.-China agreement of 1978 are discussed in Fingar and Reed (1982).

Nevertheless, the U.S. government has erected some barriers to study in this country, both through official means and by neglect. The Committee on Foreign Students and Institutional Policy (1982) notes that our national government's comparatively small-scale sponsorship of students coming from abroad has gradually weakened further over the last decade or so. Interestingly, this did not stop the overall growth of the foreign student population in the United States, since many of those arriving during the recent decade came from nations with new-found wealth. Low levels of U.S. government support may, however, act to influence the flows in the future. In any event, they probably have influenced the national composition of the foreign student population in the United States. Moreover, Winkler (1983a) notes that recent changes in funding requirements, work-study opportunities, and visa eligibility, and the ease with which visas can be adjusted have all combined to erect new obstacles to the attendance by foreign students at American colleges and universities.[11]

In summary, differences and changes in host policies toward foreign students shape the opportunities for student mobility. Some flows are facilitated while others are inhibited. Students whose access is obstructed in one place may be redirected toward another place if the latter's pull factors are sufficient. An outstanding illustration is the recent growth of Malaysian student flows to the United States and away from Britain (Goodman, 1981). Therefore, if we are adequately to plan for foreign student demands we will need to consider changes in the obstacles posed by the policies of other nations as well as those of our own.

b. By Home Governments

Home-country policies toward foreign study likewise vary considerably world-wide and can facilitate, inhibit, and shape outgoing flows of students.[12] Moreover, they often are the most unstable and unpredictable of the forces underlying transnational student mobility, because they are linked to shifts in regime and ideology (Sumra and Ishumi, 1980; Adam, 1980). For example, a government restriction on the issuance of passports in South Korea in the late 60s reduced the number of students going abroad by half, and only with its relaxation in the late 70s did the number substantially spurt upward again (Cummings, 1984). On the other hand, policy changes which seemingly should have influenced the volume of outflow in other cases, for example, changes in Taiwan in 1942 and 1977, did not have the anticipated effect (Kennedy, 1977; China Institute of America, 1954).

Except for extreme instances of isolationism, most nations do not pursue policies or take postures which restrict the outflow of students completely. Instead, the government intervenes to erect or remove obstacles for some and not others (Mashiko, 1983; Oxenham, 1981; Jacqz, 1967; Young, 1965). Thus, governments limit the choice of country and/or the institution in which their outgoing students may study. They may institute rigorous selective standards for choosing those to go abroad, or they may open study abroad to certain groups and not others. They may sponsor large numbers of students for study abroad, while limiting study abroad to those who are sponsored. They often limit the type of training that can be pursued, e.g., to undergraduate or graduate training, or to medicine, engineering, or some other field. And, they can subject potential candidates to tight foreign exchange controls or outright bonding.

The end result of these restrictions may be changes in the volume, but more often the effect is felt mainly in the composition of the student population going abroad. Thus, government interventions are more widespread in Egypt, Saudi Arabia, Kuwait, Nigeria, and Malaysia than in Japan, Hong Kong, the United Kingdom, Lebanon, Kenya, Jordan, and, until recently, Iran. We should note that all those home countries just identified as exercising greater control over foreign study are, nevertheless, represented by substantial numbers of students overseas. Their interventions do, however, alter the patterns of the student exchange, shaping the demand for one or another type of instruction. They thus can affect the hosts significantly.

The manner in which, and degree to which, a government intervenes in the educational sojourns of its citizens is frequently taken to reflect how pervasive state intervention is in the given economy and society (Oxenham, 1981; Young, 1965). Extensive state intervention geared toward development generally leads to the formation of national manpower plans. Within these plans not only the national educational system, but overseas education as well, is generally assigned a critical role. Especially for LDCs, faced as they are with internal limits on their training institutions, education abroad offers a ready means to fill gaps, enhance existing manpower, and more quickly build domestic facilities. The government therefore asserts its control over study abroad to ensure conformity to its particular developmental and ideological objectives and to regulate the use of scarce societal resources.

D. Conceptualizing and Measuring National Differences in the Level of Sending

Of course not all such policy changes are of equal concern to American educators. It depends on the numbers involved. A substantial shift in the volume or composition of students from Taiwan or Nigeria can have many more repercussions than a shift in the flow from Cyprus or Laos. Nevertheless, it would be a mistake to limit our attention to the big "senders." National differences in the use of, and reliance upon, overseas education is of interest of itself, in the case of small exporters as well as large. And these differences may not always be best measured by the number exported. Before we move on to consider research on factors underlying sending behavior, therefore, we should briefly consider alternative ways to conceptualize national differences in the level of sending.

Table 22 contains a list, for the year 1979, of some of the top national senders to the United States as measured by the absolute number of students sent. Also presented in the columns to the right are two alternative indicators of that volume for each country: the number of students sent to the United States as a proportion of the population aged 20-24 within the sending nation, and the number of students sent to the United States as a proportion of all of the sending nation's citizens enrolled in higher education at both home and abroad. The first indicator

TABLE 22

Leading National Senders of Foreign Students to the United States
by Alternative Measures of the Sending Level: 1979

Nation	Number of Students Reported	As a Percentage of Age Group 20-24	As a Percentage of All Students in Higher Education
Iran	51,310	.70%	22.00%
Taiwan	17,560	NA	NA
Nigeria	16,360	.26%	11.79%
Canada	15,130	.65%	1.74%
Japan	12,260	.15%	.50%
Hong Kong	9,900	1.74%	13.09%
Venezuela	9,860	.68%	3.15%
Saudi Arabia	9,540	1.29%	14.97%
India	8,760	.02%	.20%
Thailand	6,500	.09%	1.34%
Lebanon	6,040	2.45%	5.81%
Mexico	5,650	.09%	.68%
Korea, Rep. of	4,890	.12%	.95%
Jordan	4,720	.68%	10.46%

Sources: *Open Doors 1979/80* (IIE, 1981)
Statistical Yearbook (Unesco, 1981)

standardizes the outflow on the basis of an estimate of how many could theoretically be sent, thus yielding a measure free of the influence of population size. The second indicator is standardized on the basis of how many nationals are receiving higher education, thus providing a measure of the importance of study in the United States relative to the nation's higher education effort as a whole.

When for any country we compare the rankings on these two measures to the ranking based on absolute level, we must be struck by the substantial disagreement between the rankings. Neither alternative indicator correlates well with the original ranking. Looking first at the relation to the age group, we find, in these *relative* terms, that the flow from Lebanon exceeds that of nine nations who sent more students as measured in absolute terms to the United States. And Iran, the biggest sender in absolute terms, is only fourth and barely above Jordan, which was last among the 14 in terms of absolute level. Moreover, as List A in **Table 23** shows, the top 10 nations in relative effort include nations such as Kuwait, Libya, Guyana, Israel, and Panama, countries which do not figure among the top 15 senders on a measure of the absolute numbers sent to the United States. Hence, by looking at differences through this indicator, we can gain a sense of how much greater could the outflow of students become if larger proportions of the ultimately eligible populations were to come, or be sent, to the United States.

Relating a nation's higher education effort as a whole to its more limited activity

TABLE 23

The Top 10 Nations on Alternative Volume Measures: 1979

	Of those who send to the United States		
A		**B**	
Foreign Student Enrollment in the United States as a Percentage of Age Group 20-24		**Foreign Student Enrollment in the United States as a Percentage of All Students (Home and Abroad)**	
2.51	Kuwait	25.35	Gambia
2.45	Lebanon	22.00	Iran
1.74	Hong Kong	21.25	Guyana
1.29	Saudi Arabia	19.93	Liberia
1.21	Libya	16.09	Kuwait
.92	Guyana	15.47	Libya
.79	Israel	14.97	Saudi Arabia
.69	Panama	13.96	Ghana
.68	Venezuela	13.09	Hong Kong
.65	Canada	12.90	Jamaica

	Of those who send worldwide		
C			**D**
Foreign Student Enrollment Around the World as a Percentage of Age Group 20-24		**At Home**	**Foreign Student Enrollment Around the World as a Percentage of All Students (Home and Abroad)**
9.11	Luxembourg	(1.4)	86.71	Cyprus
7.63	Lebanon	(7.7)	86.68	Luxembourg
4.56	Greece	(29.1)	69.20	Mauritius
3.92	Kuwait	(17.8)	67.31	Laos
3.71	Mongolia	NA	52.87	Upper Volta
3.33	Hong Kong	(10.6)	46.34	Gambia
3.15	Mauritius	(1.4)	44.59	Niger
2.48	Fiji	(4.4)	41.42	Gabon
1.98	Gabon	(2.8)	41.36	Yemen
1.80	Congo	(5.4)	39.94	Benin

Sources: *Open Doors 1979/80* (IIE, 1981)
   Statistical Yearbook (Unesco, 1981)

in the United States, **Table 22** shows that Iran's 22 percent ranks highest among those in this set. However, large values are well distributed throughout the list. This tells us that quite a few nations manage to get a substantial part of all their college student population trained in the United States. List B of **Table 23** shows that Gambia, Guyana, Liberia, Kuwait, Libya, Ghana, and Jamaica all rank quite high on this indicator. For each of these, study abroad in America plays a far more critical role in its overall program for the further education of its citizens than it does for Canada, Japan, Venezuela, India, Thailand, Mexico, and South Korea, each of which sends more students *in absolute terms* to the United States.

The tendency of some countries to rely heavily on the United States to get their students educated at college level tells us more about those countries than

TABLE 24

Summary of Research on the Determinants of Sending Levels

	Winkler/Agarwal (1982)		Lee/Tan (1983)		Cummings (1984)
STUDY					
Research Design:	Cross-sectional: 1972-74; 25 eastern hemisphere LDCs; regression.		Cross-sectional; 1979; 103 LDCs; regression.		Cross-sectional; 1978; 34 Asian nations; regression.
	(1) Undergrads sent	(2) Grads sent	(1) # sent to LDCs	(2) # sent to U.S.	# students overseas per 10,000 population
Dependent Variables:	Total tertiary	Total tertiary	Total tertiary	Total tertiary	
INDEPENDENT VARIABLES:					
Domestic Education Factors					
Educational opportunities	–*	NA	–*	–*	–*
Shortage of science offerings	NA	NA	+	+*	NA
Quality (staff-student ratio)	NA	NA	+*	+*	NA
Earlier level of overseas sending	NA	NA	NA	NA	+*
Economic Factors					
Financial capacity/wealth	+*	–	+*	+*	+
Manpower needs	NA	NA	+	–	NA
Political Factor					
Political uncertainty	NA	NA	NA	NA	+
Linguistic Factor					
English as 1st or 2nd language or non-isolated by national language	+	+	NA	+*	+

Key: + = independent positive effect; – = independent negative effect; NA = not included in the study; * = independent effect was statistically significant in the study at least at the .10 level.

about the United States. List D, **Table 23,** shows that a substantial number of countries rely not just on the United States for higher education, but also use other nations as well. For example, 87 percent of the citizens of Cyprus who are enrolled in higher education are enrolled abroad. By looking at this indicator we can see that for many of these nations—Cyprus, Luxembourg, Mauritius, Gambia—study abroad is hardly transitional and supplemental. Rather, their dependency is very probably long-term. Size seems to be the key. These small nations evidently feel themselves too small to support the variety of training facilities needed by a modern society. Sending students abroad is evidently considered by them much more economical than building facilities at home.

E. Research on the "Push" to Study Abroad

In the formal testing of theories seeking to explain the number and composition of student bodies abroad the emphasis has been on push factors—in other words, on attributes of the country of origin that hold in or move out its nationals. This model may suggest more individual freedom than some assume to exist, but the facts are that very few students are ever actually officially "directed" or "sent" abroad by their governments.[13]

The few relevant cross-national quantitative studies that we are aware of all limit their attention to developing countries (Cummings, 1984; Lee and Tan, 1983; Winkler and Agarwal, 1982). Each attempts to test more rigorously a few of the conventional arguments which abound in discussions of the antecedents of going abroad to study. Many of these theories have been discussed at some point or other in this paper. They include such domestic factors as demographic pressure upon higher education, the availability of special fields and facilities, the quality of higher education provided at home, and local "traditions" of going overseas to study. Among the economic factors commonly mentioned are the ability of many nationals to meet the costs of study abroad, and the demands of the national economy for skilled manpower. Political factors often cited include uncertainty due to shifts in regime, political oppression, internal discontent, or war. A cultural factor sometimes cited is either linguistic isolation, which people seek to overcome, or a sense of affinity with some language group abroad.

Table 24 briefly describes the research design, how the "sending level" was measured, what the main push factors included in the models were, and what the findings were in each of these cross-national quantitative studies. Because there were major differences in the samples studied, the measures developed, and the dependent variables considered, the strict comparability of these studies is limited and this must temper any conclusions we may reach.[14] On the other hand, any consistent findings which emerge in spite of these differences should be noteworthy, for they attest to the probable robustness of the underlying relationship.

73

Three factors are treated in common by each of these studies: domestic opportunities to pursue further education, national wealth often measured on a per capita basis, and a linguistic factor. All three studies showed each factor to exert its effect in more or less the same way. First, lesser opportunities to pursue further education at home, as measured by the pressure of potential candidates on actual openings, was found to go with greater levels of sending. Second, greater per capita income was generally positively related to sending more students overseas. These findings should occasion little surprise. Limited opportunity pushes people to look outside; money makes it possible to go. Finally, in each study language was found to affect sending levels. Where English is the first or second language, or where citizens are not linguistically isolated by a rare national language, sending students abroad appears to be more frequent. Again, this seems a likely outcome.

Of course, in reality language functions as both a push and pull factor. As just noted, language acts most clearly as a push factor when an otherwise qualified and willing pool of students is held at home due to a rare national language. Language, nevertheless, is also a pull factor, since it constrains students' choices of where to study abroad. Some national destinations are attractive while others repel because of linguistic concerns alone. Note, however, that most often linguistic ties act only broadly to limit the options of where students may enroll. Other pull factors, and intervening obstacles, influence the *particular* choice. For example, though proficiency in English on the part of students going abroad may restrict their choices to English-speaking nations, which of these is finally chosen may well depend on such other considerations as ease of admission, cost of schooling, and program availability.

The remaining independent variables included in **Table 24** are not common to the studies but the results are still interesting. Lee and Tan examined two additional domestic education factors, the availability of science facilities and the *quality* of higher education. They found, curiously, that both the shortage of science training facilities and presence of higher quality education at home were associated with higher sending level. That is, both these conditions acted as push factors. One may assume these factors often worked in tandem. If first one provided good educational opportunity, one would train students with high expectations. But if one then failed to provide good science facilities, those same good students might be pushed to seek further training abroad.

Lee and Tan also examined the effect of how fast the economy had been growing. Such economic growth had a significant relation to student flows. The connection seems reasonable. Growth increases the need for specialists, provides jobs for trainees, and makes it easier to finance their education. Finally, Cummings (1984) examined the influence of the size of earlier student flows abroad, and of domestic political uncertainty. He found earlier flows to have a positive association with later streams. This might well be anticipated. Past flows generally continue on their own momentum, and those who earlier studied abroad provide information and models for each new generation. As for political uncertainty, Cummings found that more uncertainty led to a higher level of student outflow. One must assume that what was at work here was the effort to escape a situation in which home study was intrinsically difficult, and perhaps, personal futures were also uncertain.

We may conclude that these three efforts show that it is quite possible to test systematically a number of the existing theories which seek to account for different levels of activity in sending students abroad. They have clearly established that a number of educational, economic, political, and sociocultural factors are significantly related to those differences in level of activity.

F. What Remains to Be Done

Despite the encouraging start made in the studies we reviewed, it is obvious that much remains to be done to extend this type of quantitative investigation. We must also integrate such findings with the large number of case histories describing the interaction of government policies and local social conditions. In Venezuela, for example, reforms to improve domestic educational opportunities failed to produce an expected reduction in outflows because social values were not taken into account. The Education Ministry attempted to relieve pressure on its university sector by opening new short-term degree programs in 1970. Students largely rejected these courses, however, in favor of university study, even if getting to the university meant going abroad. They did so because the university-level degree was the only one people really valued (see Hoover, 1978). In Malaysia in 1971, the authorities adopted a policy of giving preference in college admissions to the indigenous Malays. This applied to education both at home and abroad. Nevertheless, these measures failed to help the indigenous Malays to equal or surpass the Chinese as the government intended. Chinese Malaysians reacted by increasingly going abroad on their own to study so that they could continue to compete within the home job market (Goodman, 1981). This is not a unique example, since ethnic relationships have played significant roles in shaping foreign student flows elsewhere (Cummings, 1984; Rao, 1979).

In the near future, we also should move beyond differences in level of sending, and seek to explain in more detail the national differences in the composition of the student body sent abroad. By composition, we mean whether they are largely undergraduates or graduates; whether they are destined for two-year or four-year institutions, or whether they study the humanities or engineering. Even among those countries that have sent large numbers of students to the United States, there has been considerable variation in these characteristics. For example, in 1974, 16 percent of the students from Iran were enrolled in two-year institutions, whereas only 2 percent of those coming from Taiwan were so enrolled. Looking to the contrast by grade level, we find that in 1974, 78 percent of the students from Taiwan were enrolled as graduate students, but only 30 percent of those from Nigeria were at that level. And considering field of study, in 1974, 34 percent of the students from Venezuela were studying engineering, whereas only 9 percent of the students from Canada were pursuing this area of study.

These differences highlight the variability of the demands foreign students will make on our educational institutions, depending on their countries of origin. Confronted by such striking differences, we are obviously challenged to search for systematic relationships between such variable educational patterns and the characteristics of the societies from which the students came. Winkler's and Agarwal's (1982) analysis of the undergraduate versus the graduate students sent to the United States is a step in this direction. Another is Oxenham's (1981) finding that, even for his small sample of LDCs, there is a positive relationship between national wealth and the proportion of all students who go abroad to private institutions rather than to public colleges and universities.

Does the same relationship hold if our dependent variable is the proportion attending American community or junior colleges, or if it is the proportion studying engineering? Our own exploratory correlational analysis using the most recent national data published by IIE in the *Open Doors* series (1974) suggests that such relationships do exist.[15] For example, looking at 92 cases we found a correlation between GNP per capita and the proportion enrolled in two-year institutions in the United States of − .25 (N of 92). This negative correlation would follow from the fact that school costs at the two-year level are lower than those at the college level. In addition, the kind of short-term technical preparation often sought by those from poorer countries is more frequently offered in two-year colleges. We also found for 72 LDCs that there was a correlation of .36 between GNP per capita and the proportion studying engineering in the United States. Keeping in mind that we dealt with LDCs only, the meaning we attribute to this fact is that somewhat more advanced and diversified economies come to need and value engineering more than do the poorest countries. The patterns we have illustrated and discussed throughout much of this paper suggest the likely fruitfulness of further research efforts along these lines.

Of course these kind of simple correlational finding just noted must take fuller account of the effects of forces such as government interventions which interact with these relationships. For example, with 100 countries in year 1974, we found a correlation of .44 between the proportion of students sent to the United States who were supported by the home government and the proportion studying engineering. This finding gives strong support to the idea that when governments figure prominently in paying for students to go overseas, they exert strong pressure on those students to study practical subjects related to national development goals. Indeed, this connection is so strong that it interacts in a notable way in the relationship between GNP and the study of engineering already noted above. Recall that the correlation was + .36. When we subdivided the nations into two groups of those above or below the median in the proportion self-supporting, we found that the correlation between GNP per capita and the study of engineering was much more differentiated. It was .20 (N of 50) for those below the median, and − .22 (N of 48) for those above the median. Therefore, it would appear that wealthier countries manage to get more students into engineering only if the governments involved are very active in supporting study abroad and, understandably, insist the studies they support have potential for contributing to national economic development. In the *absence* of such government intervention, however, students from the wealthier countries evidently choose engineering much less often.

Finally, we cannot leave a discussion of what kinds of research need to be done without noting the obvious fruitfulness of further investigation of pull factors. Distinct pull factors have been included in past research only on a limited basis. Lee and Tan (1983), for example, examined the influence of former colonial links. They found that former colonies of France still generally send a greater proportion of their students to France to study than do other nations. The same was found where the host was Britain and the senders were former British colonies. This kind of relationship would seem quite reasonable, given the similarity of educational systems in the former colonies and colonial powers, and the persistence of cultural, political, and economic ties between the colonizers and their former colonies.

Winkler and Agarwal (1982) specified two additional pull factors in their time-series analyses of the sending behavior of 15 eastern hemisphere nations. These were the cost of higher education in the United States, and the ease with which foreign students in the United States could adjust their visa status to that of immigrant. They report that, fairly consistently, the price of higher education in the United States has a depressing influence on the ratio of a nation's students studying in the United States to the size of the eligible pool at home. As for the prospects for immigration, Winkler and Agarwal report that, contrary to popular conceptions, except for those few nations experiencing severe internal strife, the ease of immigration plays very little part in attracting foreigners to study in the United States.

Looking to the future, we need to extend such rigorous efforts to analyze the role of pull factors in influencing where students going abroad *actually* enroll. By explicitly incorporating pull factors into our models of transnational student mobility, we can come to a deeper understanding of the processes generating the distribution of foreign students across host nations. Such developments will take us a long way toward understanding what the future of foreign student flows is likely to be.

IV. The Future of Foreign Student Exchanges

A. *What do the projections show?*

Social prediction is a chancy endeavor. Generally, almost as soon as the prediction is made it is proven wrong. On the basis of developments through 1980, the CFSIP, or Committee on Foreign Students and Institutional Policy (1982), projected that by the early 1990s there would be over one million foreign students in the United States. This projection generated much concern and debate.

Its implications were staggering. But the next few years have provided new data which indicate the need to reduce those earlier dramatic estimates by some 200,000 to 300,000 foreign students. **Table 25** presents the original projections of the CFSIP extended through 1990/1991. Alongside of their projection in **Table 25**, labeled as Scenario 1, are three of our own, labeled as Scenarios 2 through 4. All three additional projections were arrived at by using the same estimation technique employed by the CFSIP, but they are based upon the new data. Each is distinguished by its own distinctive scenario or set of assumptions. The assumptions underlying each scenario are described at the bottom of **Table 25**.

Our predictions for 1990/1991 in **Table 25** range from approximately 700,000 students to 830,000 students, depending upon the set of underlying assumptions. Nevertheless, each prediction is at least 200,000 students below the level originally expected by the CFSIP for the year 1990/1991. All in all, we consider the prediction of 698,000 foreign students in the United States by 1991, as projected under the assumptions of Scenario 3, to be the most likely of those shown. It is based upon a moderate future growth rate and the continued pace of withdrawal of Iranian students. This prediction of ours comes very close to that of Wallace Edgerton (1982), who has projected that the number in 1990 will be around 650,000.

What most wreaks havoc in this kind of predictive enterprise are the political and economic fortunes and misfortunes of nations. For example, few could have predicted the dramatic surge of students from the OPEC nations. IIE has estimated that 58 percent of the upward surge in the number of foreign students coming to the United States between 1969/1970 and 1979/1980 was attributable to an influx from OPEC nations. During that time, the proportion of foreign students in the United States who came from those nations rose from 19.2 percent to 35.1 percent of the total foreign cohort. Just as few, however, could have predicted the cutbacks by a handful of these countries, particularly Iran and Saudi Arabia, which began in the early 80s. Just as they contributed disproportionately to the growth of enrollments, so it appears they are contributing to a more moderate overall growth in the present and will perhaps do so in the future as well.

B. *Where might new, or more, growth come from in the future?*

Most often mentioned is the People's Republic of China. In the PRC we have the potential for staggering inflows. For instance, Fingar and Reed (1982) estimate

TABLE 25

Projections for Foreign Student Enrollment in the United States
Through 1990/91: Alternative Scenarios

Academic Year	Estimated Foreign Enrollment (in thousands)			
	Scenario 1	Scenario 2	Scenario 3	Scenario 4
1979/80	286°	286°	286°	286°
1980/81	324	312°	312°	312°
1981/82	367	326°	326°	326°
1982/83	415	359	350	361
1983/84	470	395	377	399
1984/85	532	435	409	442
1985/86	602	478	445	490
1986/87	681	526	485	544
1987/88	771	579	530	604
1988/89	804	637	580	672
1989/90	910	700	636	748
1990/91	1030	771	698	832

Scenario 1:	Assume 13.16 percent annual growth rate based upon that being the average annual rate over the five years 1975/76-1979/80. These are the figures of the Committee on Foreign Students and Institutional Policy (1982).
Scenario 2:	Assume 10.02 percent annual growth rate based upon that being the average annual rate of growth for the five years 1977/78-1981/82.
Scenario 3:	Assume that Iran's enrollment would continue to decline at a rate of 16.0 percent/year as it has averaged over the past two years, and assume that the rest would grow at a rate of 10.1 percent as they averaged over the five years 1977/78-1981/82.
Scenario 4:	Assume that enrollments from each region would grow at the rate that each region has averaged over the five years since 1977/78: Africa 10.06 percent/year, Europe 11.72 percent/year, Latin America 8.36 percent/year, Middle East 15.9 percent/year, South & East Asia 8.78 percent/year, North America 6.6 percent/year, and Oceania 5.28 percent/year.

Sources: CFSIP (1982)
Open Doors 1981/1982 (IIE, 1983)

that due to China's sharply pyramidal educational structure only about 5 percent of the six million who graduate from secondary school each year can gain access to higher education at home. That means that if as little as 10 percent should come to the United States, we would have 600,000 extra college students from abroad each year. That is very unlikely to happen. It remains true that U.S.-China student exchange is new and rests upon a tenuous foundation. Even if more Chinese are permitted to study abroad, it will be likely that they will first be felt, though gradually, in our graduate departments (Fingar and Reed, 1982). Nevertheless, the potential is obviously staggering.

Beyond the as-yet-untapped big senders, growth may be fueled by the redirection of flows of students who presently enroll in other host countries. Such redirection could come about from those hosts altering the price of education or instituting restrictions on the current flows. Such a process of redirection has already begun in a number of nations formerly located within the British sphere of influence. A large proportion of those cut off from Britain will likely try to come to the United States (and Canada). A comparable redirection of those going to France seems less likely. Both France's present policy toward overseas students and its special linguistic ties with the former French colonies would seem to inhibit any significant redirection. It appears, however, that the Soviet Union is willing to support more students from the Third World, and this could influence the pressures on the present major host countries.

C. What are the prospects for growth in student flows from countries from which the United States already is receiving students?

Present inflows from the industrialized countries are likely to remain stable and modest. The critical question, therefore, becomes one focused on the contribution of developing nations which already send the bulk of the students to the United States. Here again, much will depend on the interaction of home government policies and the domestic social processes which push students abroad. Oxenham (1981) notes that nine of the 10 LDCs he studied anticipated increased use of study abroad in the immediate future. In all likelihood, most developing countries will not be able to substantially close the gap between the number of aspiring students produced by the secondary schools and the number of openings in their systems of higher education. Moreover, further expansion of secondary schooling may well occur in such nations as Afghanistan, Pakistan, Saudi Arabia, and Thailand, as noted by Cummings (1984). If that happens, it will probably sustain and enlarge the flows of students going abroad. Finally, we must weigh the potential effect of the rising standard of living in many countries. As IIE noted in 1982, there is a strong propensity for middle-income countries to send students abroad. Other studies show a positive influence of a nation's level of economic development on its tendency to send students abroad. We should, therefore, anticipate expanded numbers of students from those Third World nations which will achieve economic growth in the years ahead. This means more inflow from a number of Asian nations, such as Hong Kong, Korea, Thailand, and Taiwan, and probably less growth in students from most African nations.

Underlying such changes, however, will most likely be the continuation of flows of students from such nations as Taiwan, Japan, India, and Canada. The flows of students from these countries to the United States have relatively long traditions and are backed by well-established international ties which suggest for them a less volatile, even if expanding, flow of student exchange in the future.

FOOTNOTES

1. Overall, the data on worldwide student exchanges are less complete and reliable than those available for the United States alone. Unesco's annual yearbook has regularly included some data on foreign students, although the breadth of its offerings has declined over the past 10 years. Moreover, Unesco's special studies on students abroad have not, to our knowledge, been updated since 1973. The figures we draw from these sources and present here should be treated as estimates and should be cautiously used. For a further elaboration, refer to Unesco (1981; III-2, III-461 to III-491) and Unesco (1976; 7-22).

2. It would be reasonable to expect that such cross-peripheral exchange might be more advantageous to all parties involved, because of cost considerations and common needs and problems. Yet, language and cultural differences, as well as dependence on core countries, appear to continue to obstruct this development. Intraregional exchange within the developing world is more frequent and holds promise when centers within regions can be built up. For example, see the experience of the Arab countries in the Middle East which use the Egyptian universities a great deal.

3. Systematic worldwide data on numbers of foreign students pursuing each of these fields has only been collected and published by Unesco in the *Students Abroad* series for the years 1962, 1968, and 1973.

4. For U.S. data we use the definition of foreign student adopted in IIE's *Open Doors* series. Thus, a foreign student is defined as anyone who is enrolled in courses in the United States who is not a citizen or a permanent immigrant; refugees are included. For further details of the IIE data-gathering techniques, we refer the reader to this series.

5. The U.S.S.R., for which no data were available, was probably in third place as a host to foreign students.

6. To an extent, referring to two-year institutions as independent destinations is misleading, though at present there is no accurate means to determine how misleading. This is true because initial destination may not be equivalent to ultimate destination. For example, Diener's (1978) preliminary effort indicates that though 72 percent of the students studied who were attending two-year institutions had entered directly from the home country, 28 percent had transferred at some earlier point from some four-year institution.

7. Relevant here would be a consideration of how foreign student selections may be less influenced by the distance from home, a factor which may come into play for American students. Dependence upon financial aid may be different for U.S. and foreign students. A number of private schools might have an edge in reputation and drawing power. Furthermore, differences in aggressiveness of recruitment and institutionalization of "recruiting" policies between public and private schools would need to be considered.

8. Our computations for the academic year 1981/82 using the data collected by IIE yields an ordering identical to that found by Diener, although the exact proportions differ.

9. We should note here that in four of eight fields surveyed by IIE (1981) in *Profiles,* the majority of foreign students were found to be pursuing studies at the graduate level. These four were agriculture, education, the natural and life sciences, and the social sciences.

10. Kaplan (1983:257) prefaces his discussion of "sending" behavior by acknowledging the difficulty of this task when he states, ".... it would be fair to say that the flow and distribution of foreign students are conditioned by every change in political and economic events around the world."

11. To the extent a part of the flow of students to the United States represents a shadow immigration

system, any future changes in immigration laws may have important consequences for the future student flows to the United States.

12. Studies of home-country policies have usually been conducted for a limited geographical area and have concentrated on the policies of developing countries. For reviews of policies in the Middle East, see Young (1965); for policies of African nations see Moock (1984), Sumra and Ishumi (1980), Kinyanjui, et al., (1980), Koloko (1980), Adam (1980), Similane (1980), and Jacqz (1967); for policies of some Asian nations, see Cummings (1984), Fingar and Reed (1982), Goodman (1981), Kennedy (1977), and the China Institute of America (1954); for somewhat broader reviews of policies, see Ellen Mashiko's chapter in Jenkins (1983) and Oxenham (1981).

13. Most students going abroad are not sent in the sense they are "officially" sponsored by the home government. The research of IIE indicates that approximately 85 percent of the students arriving in the United States have not received any financial resources from within their own country other than that received from their own families (IIE, 1981). Our own research, based on the data published in the *Open Doors* series, indicates that the average government supports under 10 percent of its nationals studying in the United States. To what extent then can we say these students are "sent" by their respective nations? Here we follow Cummings (1984) in arguing that the individual calculus in the decision to go abroad is prompted and conditioned by the national context within which the student is located. Hence the use of "sent" here is to connote "pushed."

14. Some critics would say these studies are marred by substantial conceptual and methodological problems. We feel this report is not the appropriate place to elaborate a criticism, nor to mount a defense, of these studies. We view them as interesting, indeed pioneering, explorations in a program of research that is barely begun.

15. Throughout these exploratory analyses we followed the rule of including only those countries which were represented by at least 20 students in the United States at that time. Otherwise, the proportions may well be meaningless.

REFERENCES

Adam, H. M.
1980   "Somali Policies Towards Education, Training and Manpower." Pp. 99-122 in T.L. Mali-yamkono (ed.), *Policy Developments in Overseas Training*. Dar es Salaam: Black Star Agencies.

Blaug, Mark
1981   "The Economic Costs and Benefits of Overseas Students." Pp. 47-90 in Peter Williams (ed.), *The Overseas Student Question*. London: Heinemann.

Burn, Barbara B.
1978   *Higher Education Reform: Implications for Foreign Students*. New York: Institute of International Education.

China Institute in America
1954   *A Survey of Chinese Students in American Universities and Colleges in the Past One Hundred Years*. New York: China Institute in America.

Coleman, James S.
1984   "Professional Training and Institution Building in the Third World: Two Rockefeller Foundation Experiences." *Comparative Education Review* 28(2):180-202.

Committee on Educational Interchange Policy
1963   *Women in Educational Exchange with the Developing Countries.* New York: Institute of
            International Education.
1961   *Educational Exchange in the Economic Development of Nations.* New York: Committee
            on Educational Interchange Policy.
1960   *African Students in the United States.* New York: Committee on Educational Interchange
            Policy.
1957   *Expanding University Enrollments and the Foreign Student: A Case for Foreign Students
            at U.S. Colleges and Universities.* New York: Committee on Educational Interchange Policy.

Committee on Foreign Students and Institutional Policy
1982   *Foreign Students and Institutional Policy.* Washington, D.C.: American Council on Edu-
            cation.

Cummings, William K.
1984   "Going Overseas for Higher Education: The Asian Experience." *Comparative Education
            Review* 28(2):241-257.

Diener, Thomas
1980   "Foreign Students and U.S. Community Colleges." *Community College Review* 7(4):58-65.
1978   "Profile of Foreign Students in United States Community and Junior Colleges." Pp. 14-31
            in Edmund J. Gleazer Jr., et al., (eds.), *The Foreign Student in United States Community
            and Junior Colleges.* New York: College Entrance Examination Board.

Edgerton, Wallace
1982   "Number of Foreign Students Continues to Increase but at Slower Pace." *Change*
            14(November/December):49-51.

Eide, Ingrid, ed.
1970   *Students As Links Between Cultures.* Oslo: Universitets-forlaget.

Fingar, Thomas and Linda A. Reed
1982   *An Introduction to Education in the People's Republic of China and U.S.–China Edu-
            cational Exchanges.* Washington, D.C.: Committee on Scholarly Communication with the
            People's Republic of China and the National Association for Foreign Student Affairs.

Fry, Gerald W.
1984   "The Economic and Political Impact of Study Abroad." *Comparative Education Review*
            28(2):203-220.

Goodman, Norman Gordon
1981   The Institutionalization of Foreign Education and the Effects of the Charter: A Study of
            Malaysian Student Attitudes and Adjustment to Overseas Educational Opportunity. Ph.D.
            dissertation, School of Education, Stanford University.

Goodwin, Craufurd D. and Michael Nacht
1983   *Absence of Decision: Foreign Students in American Colleges and Universities: A Report on
            Policy Formation and Lack Thereof.* New York: Institute of International Education.

Grafton, Clive
1970   "Foreign Student Patterns in American Community Colleges." *Junior College Journal*
            40(6):32-33.

Halls, W. D.
1971   *International Equivalences in Access to Higher Education.* Paris: Unesco.

Hoover, Gary
1978   *Venezuela: A Study of the Educational System of Venezuela and a Guide to the Academic
            Placement of Students from Venezuela in Educational Institutions of the U.S.* Washington,
            D.C.: AACRAO.

Hunter, Guy
1981   "The Needs and Desires of Developing Countries for Foreign Study Facilities: Some
            Reflections." Pp. 135-149 in Peter Williams (ed.), *The Overseas Student Question*. London:
            Heinemann.

Institute of International Education
1981   *Profiles: The Foreign Student in the United States*. New York: Institute of International
            Education.
Annual   *Open Doors: Report on International Educational Exchange*. New York: Institute of
            International Education.

Jacqz, Jane W.
1967   *African Students at U.S. Universities*. New York: The African-American Institute.

Jenkins, Hugh M., et al
1983   *Educating Students from Other Nations*. San Francisco: Jossey-Bass.

Kaplan, Robert B.
1983   "Meeting the Educational Needs of Other Nations." Pp. 253-276 in Hugh M. Jenkins, et al.,
            (eds.), *Educating Students from Other Nations*. San Francisco: Jossey-Bass.

Kennedy, Patrick J.
1977   *Republic of China: A Study of the Educational System of the Republic of China and a
            Guide to the Academic Placement of Students in Educational Institutions of the U.S.*
            Washington, D.C.: AACRAO.

Kinyanjui, K., M. Adholla, and P. Anaminyi
1980   "Evolution of Overseas Training in Kenya." Pp. 58-79 in T.L. Maliyamkono (ed.), *Policy
            Developments in Overseas Training*. Dar es Salaam: Black Star Agencies.

Koloko, E. M.
1980   "Origins of Overseas Training for Zambians 1900-1975." Pp. 80-98 in T.L. Maliyamkono
            (ed.), *Policy Developments in Overseas Training*. Dar es Salaam: Black Star Agencies.

Lee, Everett S.
1966   "A Theory of Migration." *Demography* 3(1):47-57.

Lee, Kiong Hock and Jee Peng Tan
1983   "The International Flow of Third Level LDC Students to DC's: Determinants and Impli-
            cations." Education Department, The World Bank (mimeographed paper).

Maliyamkono, T. L.
1980   "Are Overseas Scholarships a Question of Economics?" Pp. 60-68 in A.G.M. Ishumi and
            T.L. Maliyamkono (eds.), *Education and Social Change*. Dar es Salaam: Black Star Agencies.

Maliyamkono, T. L. and S. Wells
1980   "Impact Surveys on Overseas Training." Pp. 1-37 in T.L. Maliyamkono (ed.), *Policy De-
            velopments in Overseas Training*. Dar es Salaam: Black Star Agencies.

Margolis, Alan M.
1977   *Nigeria: A Study of the Educational System of Nigeria and A Guide to the Academic
            Placement of Students in Educational Institutions of the U.S.* Washington, D.C.: AACRAO.

Moock, Joyce Lewinger
1984   "Overseas Training and National Development Objectives in Sub-Saharan Africa." *Com-
            parative Education Review* 28(2):221-240.

National Center for Education Statistics
1982   *Digest of Education Statistics 1982*. Washington, D.C.: National Center for Education
            Statistics.

Oxenham, John
1981   "Study Abroad and Development Policy—An Enquiry." Pp. 150-164 in Peter Williams (ed.),
            The Overseas Student Question. London: Heinemann.

Rao, G. Lakshmana
1979   *Brain Drain and Foreign Students*. New York: St. Martin's Press.

Similane, V. M.
1980   "Analysis of Training Policies in Swaziland." Pp. 123-130 in T.L. Maliyamkono (ed.), *Policy Developments in Overseas Training*. Dar es Salaam: Black Star Agencies.

Slocum, Joel B.
1969   *Iran: A Study of the Educational System and Guide to the Admission and Academic Placement of Iranian Students in Colleges and Universities in the U.S.* Washington, D.C.: AACRAO.

Smith, Alan, Christine Woesler de Panafieu, and Jean-Pierre Jarousse
1981   "Foreign Student Flows and Policies in an International Perspective." Pp. 165-222 in Peter Williams (ed.), *The Overseas Student Question*. London: Heinemann.

Spaulding, Seth and Michael J. Flack
1976   *The World's Students in the United States*. New York: Praeger.

Sumra, S. A. and A. G. Ishumi
1980   "Trends in Tanzania's Policies Towards Higher Training." Pp. 38-57 in T.L. Maliyamkono (ed.), *Policy Developments in Overseas Training*. Dar es Salaam: Black Star Agencies.

Unesco
Annual   *Statistical Yearbook*. Paris: Unesco.
1976   *Statistics of Students Abroad 1969-1973*. Paris: Unesco.
1971   *Statistics of Students Abroad 1962-1968*. Paris: Unesco.

Wallace, William
1981   "Overseas Students: the Foreign Policy Implications." Pp. 111-134 in Peter Williams (ed.), *The Overseas Student Question*. London: Heinemann.

Weiler, Hans N.
1984   "The Political Dilemmas of Foreign Study." *Comparative Education Review* 28(2):168-179.

Wheeler, W. Reginald, Henry H. King, and Alexander B. Davidson
1925   *The Foreign Student in America*. New York: Association Press.

Williams, Peter
1981   "Overseas Students in Britain: the Background." Pp. 22-46 in Peter Williams (ed.), *The Overseas Student Question*. London: Heinemann.
1981   *The Overseas Student Question: Studies for a Policy*. London: Heinemann.

Winkler, Donald R.
1983a   "The Costs and Benefits of Foreign Students in United States Higher Education." *Journal of Public Policy* 4:115-138.
1983b   "The Fiscal Consequences of Foreign Students in Public Higher Education: a Case Study of California." *Economics of Education Review* Vol. 3.

Winkler, Donald R. and Vinod B. Agarwal
forthcoming "Foreign Demand for United States Higher Education: A Study of Developing Countries in the Eastern Hemisphere." *Economic Development and Cultural Change*.

Young, Robert Lee
1965   Study Abroad and National Purpose in the Middle East. Ph.D. dissertation, School of Education, Stanford University.

3.
Flows, Costs, and Benefits of Foreign Students in the United States:

Do We Have a Problem?

LEWIS C. SOLMON
RUTH BEDDOW
University of California, Los Angeles

Prepared for the Institute for International Education (IIE)
Conference on Foreign Students on U.S. Campuses,
Wayzata, Minnesota, April 13–15, 1984

Introduction

Even though the current 2.7 percent enrollment share of foreign students in the U.S. postsecondary student population may be minimal, the absolute growth of foreign students in the United States has been dramatic; there were fewer than 75,000 foreign students in the United States in 1963-64, and only a third that many in 1950; in 1983, there were 337,000. The possibility of further rapid growth[1] has stimulated discussion of appropriate policy, which has considered everything from impacts on individual domestic and foreign students to the effects of foreign students on the domestic security, foreign policy, and economic growth of the United States.

Somewhere in the middle of these concerns has been the impact of foreign students on American colleges and universities. Clearly, that impact varies. The top five recipient institutions of foreign students hosted 16,285 of them in 1982/83, which was about 5 percent of the total and about 10 percent of their respective student bodies. Seventy institutions had over 1,000 foreign students each, with individual campus shares ranging from 3 to 25 percent (Scully, 1983).

Later in this paper, we shall discuss the variety of positive and negative impacts foreign students are alleged to have on American colleges and universities. But the potential significance of foreign students can be illustrated by one particular set of statistics. National Center for Educational Statistics (NCES) projections indicate that between 1980/81 and 1988/89, full-time domestic enrollments are

TABLE 1

Foreign Student Enrollment by Field of Study[1]

		1949/50	1954/55	1959/60	1963/64	1969/70	1973/74	1979/80	1981/82	GROWTH 1949/81
Total Foreign Students	Number	26,433	34,232	48,486	74,814	134,959	151,066	286,340	326,300	12.34
Agriculture	Percent	4.3		3.3	3.1	2.7	2.8	3.0	2.8	8.04
	Number	1,137		1,600	2,319	3,644	4,230	8,590	9,136	
Business-Management	Percent	8.3		8.5	8.5	11.5	14.4	15.9	17.9	26.62
	Number	2,194		4,121	6,359	15,520	21,754	45,528	58,408	
Education	Percent	5.3		5.1	5.4	5.8	4.6	4.8	4.6	10.71
	Number	1,401		2,473	4,040	7,828	6,949	13,744	15,010	
Engineering	Percent	19.5		23.3	22.5	22.0	23.8	25.0	23.1	14.62
	Number	5,154		11,297	16,833	29,691	35,954	71,585	75,375	
Fine Arts	Percent	4.4		5.0		4.7		4.5	4.9	13.75
	Number	1,163		2,424		6,343		12,885	15,989	
Health	Percent	9.3		7.6	6.8	4.4	6.6	3.9	4.1	5.44
	Number	2,458		3,685	5,087	5,938	9,970	11,167	13,378	

Humanities/ Fine Arts	**Percent**	16.3	15.4	19.8	14.1	19.9	9.5	9.3	7.04
	Number	4,309	7,467	14,813	19,029	30,062	27,202	30,346	
Mathematics/ Computer	**Percent**		2.1		3.3		4.8	6.4	20.51
	Number		1,018		4,454		13,744	20,883	
Physical Sciences	**Percent**	7.9	12.9	17.7	12.6	15.0	8.3	7.3	11.41
	Number	2,088	6,255	13,242	17,005	22,660	23,766	23,820	
Social Science	**Percent**	8.7	11.9	15.4	11.7	12.6	9.1	8.7	13.34
	Number	2,300	5,770	11,521	15,790	19,034	26,057	28,388	
Other	**Percent**	20.4	6.8	0.8	7.1	0.3	6.5	8.2	4.96
	Number	5,392	3,297	599	9,582	453	18,612	26,757	
Intensive English	**Percent**						2.4	3.1	
	Number						6,872	10,115	
Undeclared	**Percent**		3.1		4.8		6.8	4.5	9.56
	Number		1,503		6,478		19,471	14,683	

1. Percentages given are of total enrollment.

Source: *Profiles* (IIE, 1983: **Tables 6.6** and **3.2**)

likely to fall by 1,075,000 at the undergraduate level, and by 130,000 at the graduate level (NCES, 1982). If there were no compensating increase in foreign student enrollments, assuming an undergraduate student/faculty ratio of 20:1 and a graduate student/faculty ratio of 10:1 (this roughly approximates Cartter, 1976), over 66,000 fewer faculty would be required in 1989 than at the beginning of the decade. Those institutions facing the greatest decline in domestic enrollments clearly have a strong incentive to attract a disproportionate number of the new foreign students, and to stimulate foreign enrollments even beyond what has been projected.[2]

If this inferred incentive is correct, we may observe a classic case of the economist's fallacy of composition: What is good for the individual institution may not be good for the system as a whole. That judgment awaits our analysis of the full set of costs and benefits deriving from foreign students in the United States. It also depends upon which institutions and fields of study will experience the greatest declines in domestic enrollments (probably low-quality schools and nontechnical fields; Solmon, 1981), and it requires the separation of institutional self-interest from broader issues of state and national concern.

Foreign Student Flows

Enrollment Trends

The impact of foreign students on American colleges and universities, and on the nation more generally, can only be assessed through disaggregating available data by field and degree level. An influx of 100,000 more foreign undergraduates will have no effect on the demand for humanities faculty if all the students enroll in science and engineering. The shortage of computer science faculty will not be solved by a growth in computer science doctoral students, if all the growth is from foreign students who intend to return to their native countries upon graduation. Therefore, this section will review trend data which are available on foreign students by field and degree level.

Two types of statistics will be considered. First we shall look at changes over time in the numbers of foreign students. More useful for some purposes, however, are figures on share of all U.S. students who are foreign. The latter enables us to discuss the impact of foreigners on various fields at various degree levels.

The Institute of International Education (IIE) has developed data on the numbers of foreign students separately by field and degree level from 1950 to 1982. IIE does not provide comparable data on domestic students, so their figures are useful only to look at magnitudes of foreign students, not at impact on various fields at various degree levels.

Table 1 shows that between 1949/50 and 1981/82, the number of foreign students in this country grew by a factor of over 12, from 26,433 to 326,300. The most popular two fields in 1950 for foreign students were engineering (19.5 percent) and the humanities (11.9 percent), followed by health-related fields (9.3 percent) and the social sciences (8.7 percent). By 1981/82, business became the second most popular field for foreign students (17.9 percent) after engineering, which was still most popular at 23.1 percent. Social science majors were third most frequently chosen (8.7 percent), but the humanities fell in popularity to 4.4 percent.[3]

Another way of looking at these trends is to compare the magnitude of growth of foreign students in various fields to the overall growth rate of 12.34 times over the 32-year period. Growth was greatest in the fields of business (26.62 times), engineering (14.62 times), fine arts (13.75 times), and the social sciences (13.34 times). The data on math/computer science begin only in 1959/60, but from then to 1981/82, the growth was 20.51 times. Physical science grew by only 11.41 times, less than the growth of total foreign students; however, apparently in the earliest years the physical science figures included mathematics. In all likelihood, the physical sciences excluding mathematics grew at a rate greater than the overall rate as well. Relatively slow-growing disciplines were the humanities (4.56 times), health fields (5.44 times), agriculture (8.04 times), education (10.71 times), and other and unspecified fields (between five and nine times).

The most spectacular growth has occurred in the field of business. Engineering grew the most in absolute numbers, but its great popularity even in the 1950s prevented the growth rate from being as high as business. Other than fine arts, all the above average growth has occurred in the sciences and engineering or in business. The humanities, health, agriculture, and education have shown the smallest relative growth.

TABLE 2

Foreign Student Enrollment by Level[1]

	1954/55	1959/60	1963/64	1969/70	1973/74	1979/80	1981/2
Undergraduate							
Percentage	57.2	53.0	48.2	48.5	50.4	58.1	59.7
Number	19,581	25,698	36,060	65,455	76,137	166,364	194,801
Graduate							
Percentage	36.2	39.6	41.9	45.3	44.3	35.9	35.2
Number	12,392	19,200	31,347	61,136	66,922	102,796	114,858
Other							
Percentage	6.6	7.4	9.9	6.2	5.3	6.0	5.1
Number	2,259	3,588	7,407	8,367	8,006	17,180	16,641

1. *Percentages given are of total foreign enrollment.*

Source: *Profiles* (IIE, 1983: **Tables 6.6** and **4.3**)

TABLE 3
Foreign Student Enrollment by Level and Field of Study

		1963/64		1969/70	
		Percent	**Number**	**Percent**	**Number**
TOTAL		100	74,814	100	134,959
Agriculture	UG	1.1	823	0.8	1,080
	GR	1.7	1,272	1.9	2,564
	OTH	0.3	224	0.2	270
Business	UG	5.0	3,740	7.3	9,852
	GR	2.7	2,020	4.1	5,533
	OTH	0.8	599	0.7	945
Education	UG	2.5	1,870	2.7	3,644
	GR	2.2	1,646	3.0	4,049
	OTH	0.7	524	0.3	405
Engineering	UG	13.1	9,801	11.2	15,115
	GR	8.2	6,135	11.0	14,845
	OTH	1.2	898	0.8	1,080
Health	UG	3.1	2,319	2.4	3,239
	GR	2.8	2,095	1.9	2,564
	OTH	0.9	673	0.4	540
Humanities	UG	10.3	7,706	11.3	15,250
	GR	5.7	4,264	6.1	8,232
	OTH	3.8	2,843	3.2	4,319
Physical Science	UG	6.3	4,713	5.6	7,558
	GR	10.6	7,930	10.4	14,036
	OTH	0.8	599	0.7	945
Social Science	UG	6.2	4,638	5.7	7,693
	GR	8.0	5,985	6.9	9,312
	OTH	1.2	898	0.9	1,215
Other	UG	0.6	449	0.4	540
	GR				
	OTH	0.2	150	0.1	135

Source: *Profiles* (IIE, 1983: **Table 6.6**)

Two points come immediately to mind from these figures. First, *interest by domestic students has plummeted most dramatically in the humanities and education.* These are precisely the fields of low interest to foreign students. Given their small setup costs, humanities and education are probably the first disciplines to be developed by institutions in nations trying to set up their own systems of higher education. Moreover, other countries are probably least inclined to subsidize study abroad in these fields, given their perceived greater need to acquire scientific and technical knowledge. Second, *the fields in greatest demand by foreign students are both in high demand domestically, and relatively expensive to teach from the university's perspective.*

Table 2 shows that the distribution between undergraduate and graduate study of foreign students has changed little over time. The share of all foreign students

TABLE 3 (cont'd)

1973/74		1979/80		1981/82	
Percent	**Number**	**Percent**	**Number**	**Percent**	**Number**
100	151,066	100	286,340	100	326,300
0.8	1,209	1.4	4,009	1.3	4,242
1.9	2,870	1.7	4,868	1.5	4,895
0.1	151	0.1	286		
9.4	14,200	10.4	29,779	12.5	40,788
4.7	7,100	5.4	15,462	5.3	17,294
0.3	453	0.3	859	0.3	979
1.7	2,568	2.0	5,727	1.9	6,200
2.7	4,079	2.7	7,731	2.6	8,406
0.2	302	0.1	286	0.1	326
12.2	18,430	17.2	49,250	15.4	50,250
10.7	16,164	7.2	20,616	7.0	22,841
0.9	1,360	0.3	859	0.3	979
4.4	6,647	2.3	6,586	2.4	7,831
2.0	3,021	1.6	4,581	1.6	5,221
0.2	302	0.1	286	0.1	326
11.0	16,617	8.7	24,912	8.5	27,736
6.0	9,063	4.5	12,885	4.1	13,378
2.9	4,381	0.7	2,004	0.5	1,632
5.6	8,450	6.2	17,753	7.3	23,820
9.1	13,747	6.8	19,471	6.4	20,883
0.3	453	0.3	859	0.2	653
5.0	7,553	4.4	12,599	4.6	15,010
7.2	10,877	5.3	15,176	5.5	17,947
0.4	604	0.3	859	0.2	653
0.3	453	5.5	15,749	5.6	18,273
		1.0	2,863	1.5	4,895
		3.5	10,022	3.3	10,768

who are in graduate school in the United States has fallen by only one percentage point from 36.2 percent to 35.2 percent. The remainder are primarily under-graduates with "other" designations comprising 7 percent in the 1950s and 5 percent more recently.

Published data from IIE have enabled breakdowns by both field and degree level only since 1963/64. **Table 3** shows that engineering and the humanities were the most frequently chosen majors by undergraduates in 1963/64, and by 1981/82, business moved into second place after engineering. At the graduate level, the two most popular fields in 1963/64 were the physical sciences and engineering. By 1981/82, engineering surpassed the physical sciences, but these two were still the most popular. **Table 4** shows that at both the undergraduate and graduate levels, business enrollments grew the most (10.91 and 8.56 times, respectively), with agriculture, engineering, and physical sciences growing above the average undergraduate rate, and education, agriculture, and engineering growing above the average rate for foreign graduate students.

The major surprise here is growth of foreign graduate students in education. This probably reflects the desires of many less developed countries to improve both their precollegiate schools and their university systems, and their belief that

TABLE 4

Growth in Number of Foreign Students Enrolled by Level and Field of Study

	Undergraduate Students			Graduate Students		
	1963/64	1981/82	Growth (times)	1963/64	1981/82	Growth (times)
Agriculture	823	4,242	5.15	1,272	4,895	3.85
Business	3,740	40,788	10.91	2,020	17,294	8.56
Education	1,870	6,200	3.32	1,646	8,406	5.11
Engineering	9,801	50,250	5.13	6,135	22,841	3.72
Health	2,319	7,831	3.38	2,095	5,221	2.49
Humanities	7,706	27,736	3.60	4,264	13,378	3.14
Physical Science	4,713	23,820	5.05	7,930	20,883	2.63
Social Science	4,638	15,010	3.24	5,985	17,947	3.00
Total	35,610	175,877	4.94	31,347	110,865	3.54

Source: *Profiles* (IIE, 1983: **Table 6.6**)

graduate study in the field of education is a way to achieve these goals.

All these data emphasize that engineering and the physical sciences have always been a major location of foreign students at both the undergraduate and graduate levels. The interest in the field of business by foreign students has increased dramatically, as has education at the graduate level. The reverse is true for undergraduate education. The relative position of the humanities has deteriorated significantly over time.

Foreign Students as a Share of All Students

So far, the discussion has focused solely upon foreign students. It is now time to look at foreign students relative to all students in order to see how their relative positions in different fields and degree levels have changed. Many of the effects of foreign students are inferred from the fact that their numbers in U.S. colleges have grown dramatically in recent decades. But it must be kept in mind that total enrollments, that is, enrollment of primarily domestic students, have also experienced huge increases (NCES, 1982). If the result of the combined growth of domestic and foreign students were that three of every 100 students in every classroom were foreign, the effects of foreign students probably would be minimal. But when we find that almost half the recent Ph.D.s in engineering were awarded to foreign students, the situation is quite different. Again, disaggregation is the key to discerning impact of foreign students.

The Office of Civil Rights (OCR) of the U.S. Department of Health, Education and Welfare in 1976 began providing data on foreign student enrollments relative to all enrollments. For graduate students, we were able to find data back to 1963/ 64 from the NCES *Digest of Education Statistics.* When enrollments are broken down by field, the focus has usually been on the hard sciences and professions, rather than on the social sciences and humanities. Since the available data are for the fields where more foreign students enroll, they are instructive.

Between 1976 and 1982, the share of foreign students in the United States rose from 1.9 percent to 2.6 percent (see **Table 5**). Including "unclassified" degree level students, this involved an increase of over 103,000 foreign students, or 17,000 more students per year. If these increments had been equally distributed across the top 70 institutions in terms of numbers of foreign students admitted, this would have resulted in fewer than 250 additional students each year, but, *ceteris paribus,* an expanded student body of 1,450 over the six-year period. Since domestic enrollments in many of these institutions will have declined somewhat, foreign students could be viewed as a welcome counterforce over this recent period.

Table 5 breaks this trend into its undergraduate and graduate components. Between 1976 and 1982, the number of full-time foreign undergraduates rose by 57,000 (from 1.8 percent to 2.6 percent); the number of full-time foreign graduate

TABLE 5
Enrollment by Level, Status, and Citizenship[1]

| | 1976 | | | | | |
| | Full-Time | | | Part-Time | | |
	U.S. Citizen	Non-resident Alien	TOTAL	U.S. Citizen	Non-resident Alien	TOTAL
Undergraduate						
Number	5,831,481	104,421	5,935,902	2,551,954	25,454	2,577,408
Percent	98.2	1.8	100	99.0	1.0	100
Graduate						
Number	382,491	47,348	429,839	636,520	18,772	655,292
Percent	89.0	11.0	100	97.1	2.9	100
First Professional						
Number	218,604	2,849	221,453	24,124	213	24,337
Percent	98.7	1.3	100	99.1	0.9	100
	1980					
Undergraduate						
Number	6,094,256	156,992	6,251,248	3,055,625	33,553	3,089,178
Percent	97.5	2.5	100	98.9	1.1	100
Graduate						
Number	380,823	63,372	444,195	633,837	22,589	656,426
Percent	85.7	14.3	100	96.6	3.4	100
First Professional						
Number	249,152	2,741	251,893	26,389	161	26,550
Percent	98.9	1.1	100	99.4	0.6	100

1. *Figures include Guam, Puerto Rico, Virgin Islands, and outlying areas.*

Sources: 1976 and 1978—Racial, Ethnic and Sex Enrollment: Department of Health, Education and Welfare, Office for Civil Rights (**Table 17**)
1980 and 1982—Data obtained directly from Office for Civil Rights

students rose by 23,000 (from 11.0 percent to 16.5 percent); and the number of first professional degree students remained relatively constant at about 3,000 (a 0.2 decline in share). Among part-timers, only at the graduate level did the share of foreigners rise, from 2.9 percent to 4.1 percent, reflecting an increase of 6,000 students over the six-year period. Clearly, at the graduate level the impact of foreign students is largest, and the impact has grown by the largest number of percentage points.

When considering demand for faculty at American colleges and universities, the enrollment of undergraduates swamps the enrollment of graduate students

TABLE 5 (Cont'd)

	1978 Full-Time			1978 Part-Time		
	U.S. Citizen	Non-resident Alien	TOTAL	U.S. Citizen	Non-resident Alien	TOTAL
Undergraduate						
Number	5,761,619	130,021	5,891,640	2,768,150	25,250	2,793,400
Percent	97.8	2.2	100	99.1	0.9	100
Graduate						
Number	399,793	52,960	452,753	629,976	20,421	650,397
Percent	87.6	12.4	100	96.9	3.1	100
First Professional						
Number	229,937	2,730	232,667	23,610	314	23,924
Percent	98.8	1.2	100	98.7	1.3	100
	1982					
Undergraduate						
Number	5,974,537	161,372	6,135,909	3,133,047	32,498	3,165,545
Percent	97.4	2.6	100	99.0	1.0	100
Graduate						
Number	356,092	70,500	426,592	569,051	24,505	593,556
Percent	83.5	16.5	100	95.9	4.1	100
First Professional						
Number	241,459	2,800	244,259	23,562	247	23,809
Percent	98.9	1.1	100	99.0	1.0	100

as a factor, because there are almost 10 times as many undergraduates. At the graduate level, students are more relevant as future faculty, and their numbers bear on policy, particularly in fields like science and engineering, where the fear of faculty shortages is most intense. To the extent that undergraduate majors reflect future graduate enrollments, and thus prospective new faculty, they are relevant to the same policy considerations. Thus, in order to see whether increases in foreign students create more demand for faculty, or whether they are clouding projections of future availability of new faculty in high-demand areas, we must now turn to enrollment impacts by individual fields.

The first source of data is the Cooperative Institutional Research Program (CIRP) of UCLA and the American Council on Education. **Table 6** shows the number and share of foreign students who were college freshmen in 1972 and 1983. Every field saw its share of foreign freshmen rise over this 11-year period.

TABLE 6
Freshman Enrollment by Field

	Humanities[1]	English	Biology	Business	Education	Engineering	Physical Science	Health Tech	Social Science[1]	Undeclared
1972 Total Students	253,874	24,920	60,743	241,414	113,698	113,693	63,858	165,096	121,486	71,646
Percent Foreign Students	1.5	1.16	1.59	1.69	0.7	3.28	1.79	1.6	1.24	0.92
Total Foreign Students	3,808	289	704	4,080	796	3,729	1,143	2,642	1,506	659
1983 Total Students	134,791	15,755	66,522	493,648	105,032	204,812	45,515	152,297	106,783	85,776
Percent Foreign Students	2.8	2.25	5.2	2.51	1.59	5.09	3.10	2.28	3.34	2.2
Total Foreign Students	3,774	354	3,459	12,391	1,670	10,425	1,411	3,472	3,567	1,887
Difference Between 1972 and 1983	−34	65	2,755	8,311	874	6,696	268	830	2,061	1,228
1983/1972	.53	.63	1.10	2.04	.92	1.80	.71	.92	.88	1.20

1. In 1972, political science is included in humanities; in social sciences for 1982 (for Total Students). Political science is included in social sciences for both years for Foreign Student Totals.

Source: The Cooperative Institutional Research Program (CIRP) of UCLA and the American Council of Education

Foreign students comprised from 0.7 percent of the freshman class in English to 3.28 percent in engineering in 1972. By 1983, the range was from 1.59 percent in education to 5.2 percent in biology. Given the total number of majors in various fields, these relatively small shares converted into widely disparate absolute numbers of students. Since the number of freshmen planning to major in the humanities other than English in 1983 was only 53 percent of the number in 1972, the share of foreigners in these fields rose from 1.5 percent to 2.8 percent, despite an absolute decline in the number of foreign students of 34. Those planning to major in English in 1983 were only 63 percent of the 1972 total, and so the share of foreigners rose from 1.16 percent to 2.25 percent although the absolute number of foreigners increased by only 65 in that field. The physical sciences (71 percent of the 1972 figure), social sciences (88 percent), and health tech and education (both 92 percent) also had fewer total freshmen in 1983 than in 1972. Thus, foreign freshmen in the class of 1983 comprised substantially larger

TABLE 7

Full-Time Undergraduate Foreign Student Enrollment by Field[1]

	1976		1978	1980	1982	
	Number	Percent of All Students	Percent of All Students	Percent of All Students	Number	Percent of All Students
Agriculture and Natural Resources	1,725	1.4	1.9	2.3		
Architecture and Environment	1,863	3.8	4.6		2,908	6.8
Biological Science	4,139	1.8	2.1	2.4	4,294	2.5
Business and Management	15,064	2.0	2.0	2.4	25,274	3.0
Engineering	22,010	7.1	8.3	8.1	29,098	7.4
Physical Science	3,161	3.0	3.4	3.5	3,416	3.7
Mathematics					2,449	4.4

1. *Data for agriculture and natural resources were not collected for 1982. Data for architecture and environment were not collected for 1980. Figures include Guam, Virgin Islands, Puerto Rico, and outlying areas.*

Sources: 1976 and 1978—Racial, Ethnic and Sex Enrollment: Department of Health, Education and Welfare, Office for Civil Rights (**Table 17**)
1980 and 1982—Data obtained directly from Office for Civil Rights

TABLE 8
Full-Time Graduate Foreign Student Enrollment by Field[1]

	1963/64		69/70	73/74	1976	1978	1980	1982	
	Number	Share	Share	Share	Share	Share	Share	Number	Share
Agriculture and Natural Resources	1,272	24.6	31.3	24.7	21.6	22.5	23.9		
Architecture and Environment					10.0	13.2		237 PT 1,437 FT	17.2
Biological Science					8.9	9.1	9.8	834 PT 2,891 FT	12.1
Business and Management	2,020	6.2	7.2	6.6	13.9	13.6	13.4	2,891 PT 9,556 FT	14.6
Engineering	6,135	12.5	22.8	29.6	34.2	38.7	41.5	4,608 PT 15,898 FT	42.6
Physical Science	7,930	11.7	13.5	13.3	17.2	18.3	19.9	263 PT 5,868 FT	23.3
Mathematics								696 PT 2,454 FT	38.0
Education	1,646	1.3	1.7	1.3					
Health Science	2,095	28.6	20.4	11.1					

| Humanities | 4,264 | 8.9 | 9.0 | 8.7 |
| Social Science | 5,985 | 8.9 | 7.8 | 7.3 |

1. Figures for 1963/64, 1969/70, and 1973/74 include part-time students. Figures from Office for Civil Rights include Guam, Puerto Rico, Virgin Islands, and outlying areas.

Sources: 1963/64, 1969/70, 1973/74—*Digest of Educational Statistics*, National Center for Educational Statistics, 1965 edition (**Table 57**); 1945 edition (**Table 87**); 1970 edition (**Table 93**)
1976 and 1978—*Racial, Ethnic and Sex Enrollment*: Department of Health, Education and Welfare, Office for Civil Rights (**Table 17**)
1980 and 1982—Data obtained directly from Office for Civil Rights
Numbers of foreign students taken from **Table 3**

shares of the majors in all these fields, despite relatively small absolute number increases. The increase in absolute numbers of foreign freshmen and the changing shares in these fields were as follows: physical sciences 268, from 1.79 percent to 3.1 percent; social sciences 2,061, from 1.24 percent to 3.34 percent; health tech 830, from 1.6 percent to 2.28 percent; and education 874, from 0.7 percent to 1.59 percent.

The remaining fields grew overall, and so the representation of foreign students grew even faster in order that their share of the total rose. These included biology, where the number of foreigners in the freshman class of 1983 was 2,755 greater than in 1972, and the share rose from 1.59 percent to 5.2 percent. In business, the absolute increase in foreign freshmen was 8,311, resulting in a share increase from 1.69 percent to 2.51 percent. Engineering saw its number of foreign students rise by 6,696 and the share of foreign freshmen grow from 3.28 to 5.09 percent.

What is clear from these figures is that foreign students mostly were entering those fields that were growing in popularity with American students as well. Any hope that foreigners will play a major role in filling the empty seats in fields hit by both declining popularity and the end of the baby boom seems to be overly optimistic.

The OCR data enable us to look at the total full-time undergraduate students by field, although not for all fields, and only between 1976 and 1982. The data are presented in **Table 7**. It is apparent that except for architecture/environmental studies, whose share of foreign students rose from 3.8 percent to 6.8 percent, no field saw its share increase by more than one percentage point. It is noteworthy, however, that the number of full-time foreign undergraduates in business and management rose by 10,000 in this six-year period, and the number of foreign students in engineering grew by 7,000.

At the graduate level, data are less consistent, although we can look as far back as 1963/64 in some fields. We do know from **Table 8** that foreign students in agriculture and natural resources maintained a share in the mid-20s-percent range while their absolute numbers more than doubled between 1963/64 and 1982. The share of foreign students in business and management rose from 6.2 percent to 14.6 percent (7,000 students) over the same period. Despite an absolute decline of 2,000 students, the share of foreign students in the physical sciences rose from 11.7 percent to 23.3 percent. The share of foreign students in mathematics in 1982 was 38 percent. Since no reporting of this field was provided for earlier years, it might have been included in physical sciences. If this is the case, probably the number of foreign students has remained constant and the share has increased by even more than reported for the physical sciences.

The most dramatic story at the graduate level is in engineering. In 1963/64, there were 6,135 foreign graduate students in that field and they comprised 12.5 percent of all enrolled. That share has risen steadily, until by 1982 there were 15,898 foreign full-time graduate students in engineering who made up 42.6 percent of the total! In addition, there were 4,600 part-time foreign graduate students in engineering.

Since (1) overall graduate enrollments of foreign students have risen only from 11 percent to 16.5 percent since 1976, (2) agriculture has always had a large share but small absolute numbers of foreign students, and (3) the large growth in foreign business students still results in a share below the total, the situation in engineering is unique. Indeed, we believe that the prospect (fear) of foreigners soon becoming the majority of graduate students in engineering is the single fact which has caused the furor over foreign students in this country.

Engineering is clearly a strategic, pivotal discipline in terms of our national productivity concerns, our international economic position, and even national defense. Engineering education is highly capital-intensive, and so has the greatest capacity constraints of all disciplines. The cost of training engineers is greater than that of training people in virtually all other fields. Tuition is rarely differentiated by field of study. Demand for engineers in the United States today is such that most who complete undergraduate programs are lured away from further study into high-paying jobs. Thus, engineering departments are unable to replace faculty who retire or leave academe, to say nothing of being able to add new faculty to meet expansion needs. And demand for engineers abroad makes it very unlikely that foreign graduates will remain in the United States to help solve some of our manpower requirements.

The most ardent nationalists might resent training our economic and scientific competitors under any circumstances; when foreign engineering students are seen as taking away spots from Americans, even if the latter are marginally less "qualified," policy changes are urged upon us. However, the most important fact

TABLE 9

Bachelor's Degrees Awarded by Field

| | 1963/64 | 1973/74 | 1978/79 | | 1980/81 | | 1988/89 | |
	Total	Total	Total	Nonresident	Total	Nonresident	Total	Nonresident
Agriculture and Natural Resources	6,121	16,253	23,134	479	22,033	616	28,550	1,570
Biological Science	22,808	48,340	48,794	887	44,046	903	55,030	1,634
Business and Management	56,088	132,384	172,524	3,499	203,810	4,578	192,340	6,021
Education	112,503	185,181	125,786	869	110,715	920	73,530	1,022
Engineering	33,353	50,286	61,426	4,760	75,395	6,963	76,310	11,599
Health Science	11,590	41,459	62,085	600	64,673	582	73,470	455
Humanities	70,277	134,547	106,346	1,723	103,446	2,014	83,590	2,723
Physical Science	36,159	47,569	43,294	1,433	50,581	1,965	43,030	2,659
Social Science	90,323	226,592	188,644	2,422	180,053	2,785	156,750	4,103
Other	21,245	63,165	84,314	1,431	92,125	1,305	109,200	313

Sources: *Projections of Education Statistics*, National Center for Educational Statistics, 1988/89 (**Table 18**)
Digest of Education Statistics, National Center for Educational Statistics, 1965 (**Table 73**); 1975 (**Table 112**); 1982 (**Table 109**)

105

TABLE 10

Master's Degrees Awarded by Field

	1963/64	1973/74	1978/79		1980/81		1988/89	
	Total	Total	Total	Nonresident	Total	Nonresident	Total	Nonresident
Agriculture and Natural Resources	1,344	2,928	3,994	725	4,017	710	5,120	808
Biological Science	3,297	6,552	6,831	464	6,015	368	6,570	226
Business and Management	6,375	32,753	50,043	4,388	58,192	5,052	52,200	4,346
Education	40,710	112,252	111,487	27,442	98,632	2,699	89,460	3,525
Engineering	10,827	15,379	15,239	3,952	16,716	4,563	15,930	5,222
Health Science	2,299	9,599	15,485	634	16,685	698	19,330	880
Humanities	12,002	27,922	23,662	1,382	23,002	1,778	21,900	3,348
Physical Science	8,170	13,172	11,419	1,643	12,087	2,154	12,410	3,914
Social Science	11,548	34,422	40,833	2,226	40,292	2,584	47,910	4,917
Other	4,550	20,148	20,894	1,247	21,160	1,452	28,890	3,013

Sources: *Projections of Education Statistics*, National Center for Educational Statistics, 1988/89 (**Table 18**)
Digest of Education Statistics, National Center for Educational Statistics, 1965 edition (**Table 73**); 1975 edition (**Table 112**); 1982 edition (**Table 109**)

TABLE 11
Doctoral Degrees Awarded by Field

	1963/64	1973/74	1978/79		1980/81		1988/89	
	Total	Total	Total	Nonresident	Total	Nonresident	Total	Nonresident
Agriculture and Natural Resources	555	930	950	268	1,067	343	1,060	508
Biological Science	1,625	3,439	3,542	343	3,724	289	2,760	2
Business and Management	275	983	863	163	845	161	820	161
Education	2,348	7,293	7,731	497	7,900	593	6,550	774
Engineering	1,693	3,312	2,491	867	2,561	956	2,000	949
Health Science	192	578	718	81	842	88	690	49
Humanities	1,573	4,372	3,494	278	3,287	288	2,660	318
Physical Science	3,051	4,855	4,068	697	4,125	755	3,160	726
Social Science	2,718	6,692	6,390	536	6,596	541	5,960	478
Other	460	2,159	2,417	185	2,115	190	2,290	328

Source: *Projections of Education Statistics*, National Center for Educational Statistics, 1988/89 (**Table 18**)
Digest of Education Statistics, National Center for Educational Statistics, 1965 edition (**Table 73**); 1975 edition (**Table 112**); 1982 edition (**Table 109**)

TABLE 11A

Projected Change in Numbers of Degrees Awarded to Foreign Students: 1980/81 to 1988/89

	Bachelor's			Master's			Doctoral		
	1980/81	1988/89	Change	1980/81	1988/89	Change	1980/81	1988/89	Change
Agriculture and Natural Resources	616	1,570	2.55	710	808	1.13	343	508	1.48
Biological Science	903	1,634	1.80	368	226	0.61	289	2	0
Business and Management	4,578	6,021	1.31	5,052	4,346	0.86	161	161	0.01
Education	920	1,022	1.11	2,699	3,525	1.30	593	774	1.31
Engineering	6,963	11,599	1.66	4,563	5,222	1.14	956	949	0.99
Health Science	582	455	0.78	698	880	1.26	88	49	0.55
Humanities	2,014	2,723	1.35	1,778	3,348	1.88	288	318	1.10
Physical Science	1,965	2,659	1.35	2,154	3,914	1.81	755	726	0.96
Social Science	2,785	4,103	1.47	2,584	4,917	1.90	541	478	0.88
Other	1,305	313	0.23	1,452	3,013	2.07	190	328	1.72
Total	22,631	32,099	1.42	22,058	30,199	1.36	4,204	4,293	1.02

Source: *Projections of Education Statistics*, National Center for Educational Statistics, 1988/89 **(Table 18)**

to remember is that engineering seems to be the exception.[4] Despite large absolute increases in numbers of foreign students, virtually no other field at the undergraduate or graduate level seems to be getting swamped by foreign students. Most fields where the share is high have had high shares for many years. Even business, where both numbers and share of foreign students have grown, does not seem to be a problem. There is already talk of a prospective glut of MBAs in this country (Wall Street Journal, 1983). And since well before Theory Z (Ouchi, 1981), there has been a real question about the extent to which our business schools are telling future managers much that will help them in the real world.

Data on Degrees Conferred

Degree data are more instructive for some purposes than are data on enrollments. When looking at impact at the undergraduate level, the number of students enrolled at two-year colleges should be treated differently from the number in four-year colleges, but this is sometimes not done. At the graduate level, students can slow down or speed up their progress toward the degree (and hence expand or contract annual enrollment numbers) depending upon labor market conditions. And there are often confusions between part- and full-time students, the head count versus full-time equivalent problem.

Tables 9, 10, and **11** provide data on degrees awarded by field, at the bachelor's, master's, and doctorate levels respectively, for selected years between 1963 and 1980. **Figures 1** through **4** graph the share of foreign Ph.D.s by field from 1967 to 1981 (NRC, 1968-83). These figures illustrate how unique the growth of the share of foreign doctorates in engineering has been.

Tables 9 through **11** also indicate NCES projections of numbers of each of the degrees to be awarded in 1988/89. Finally, for the years 1978/79 and 1980/81, data on degrees awarded to nonresident aliens are presented.

The final column in each table is our estimate of degrees that will be awarded to foreigners eight years from the last data point, that is, in 1988/89. This estimate was made by assuming that the average annual rate of change in percentage of degrees awarded to foreign students between 1978/79 and 1980/81 will continue in the same equal increments or decreases to 1988/89. We then calculated that share of the NCES 1988/89 projection of total degrees to be conferred to foreign students. **Table 11A** compares the actual degrees awarded in 1980/81 to foreigners to our projections for 1988/89.

Under these assumptions, the overall growth rate of foreign bachelor's degrees would be 42 percent over the eight-year period, with a range of change from a 155 percent increase in agriculture to a decline of 22 percent in health sciences. There should be a 36 percent growth in master's degrees awarded to foreign students, the range being from an increase of 90 percent in the social sciences to a decline of 39 percent in the biological sciences. Overall, growth of foreign

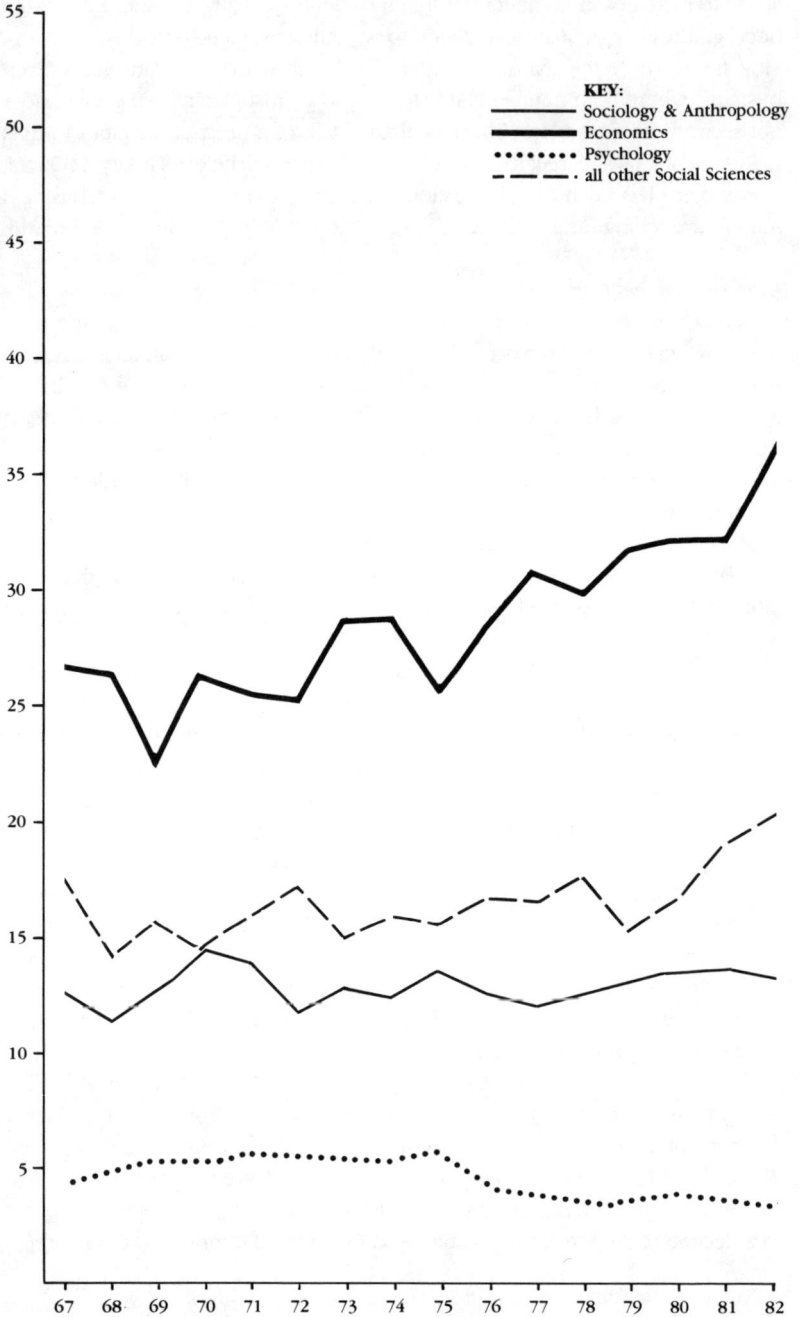

Figure 1
SOCIAL SCIENCES
Percent of Doctorates Awarded to Foreign Citizens

KEY:
———— Sociology & Anthropology
———— Economics
•••••• Psychology
— — — all other Social Sciences

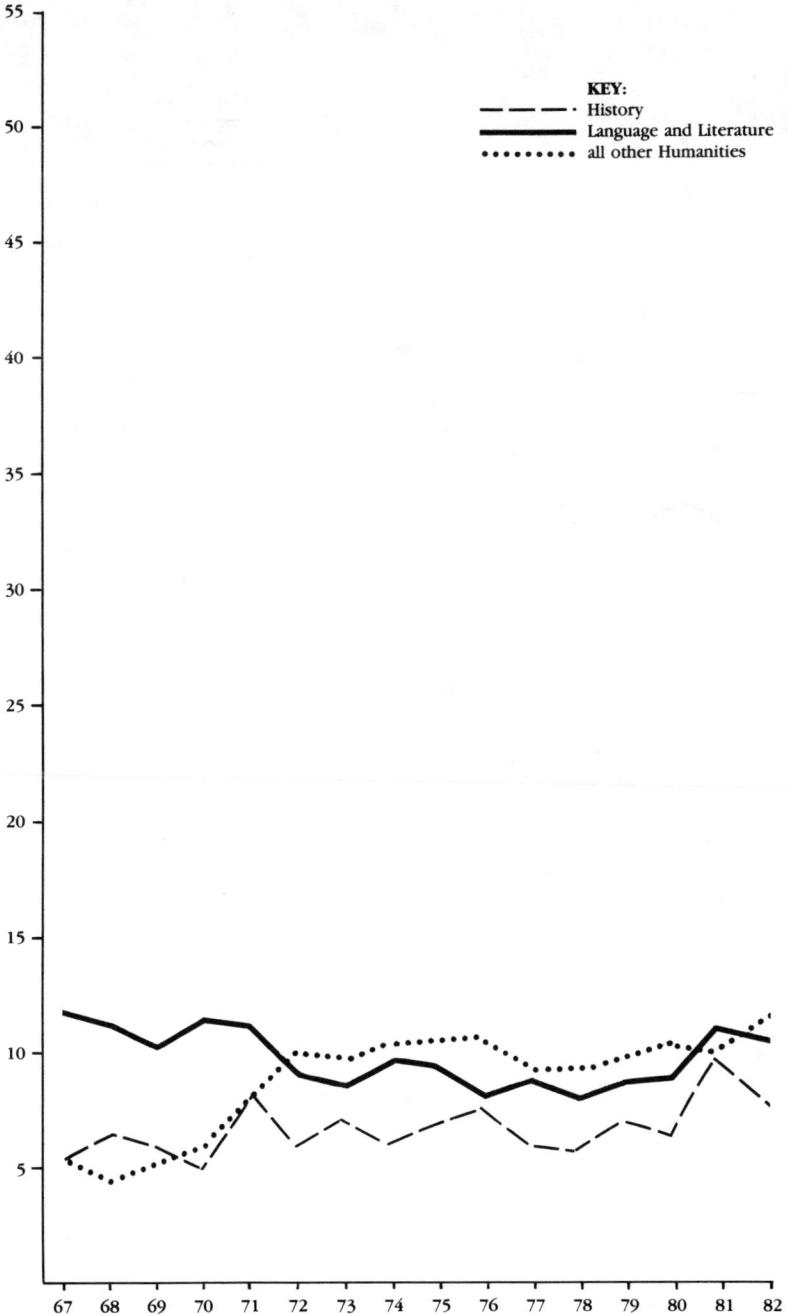

Figure 2
HUMANITIES
Percent of Doctorates Awarded to Foreign Citizens

KEY:
— — — · History
——— Language and Literature
· · · · · · · · · all other Humanities

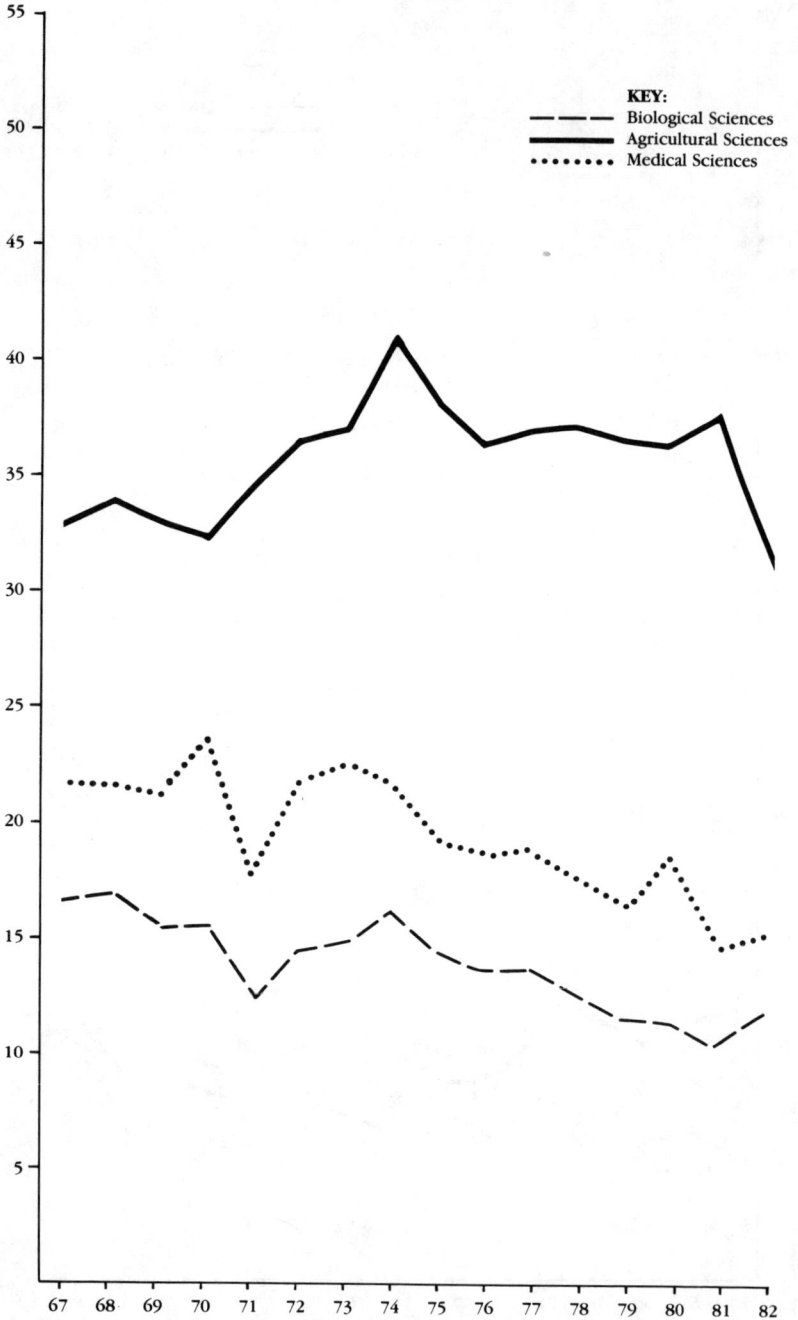

Figure 3
LIFE SCIENCES
Percent of Doctorates Awarded to Foreign Citizens

KEY:
— — — Biological Sciences
—— Agricultural Sciences
· · · · · · Medical Sciences

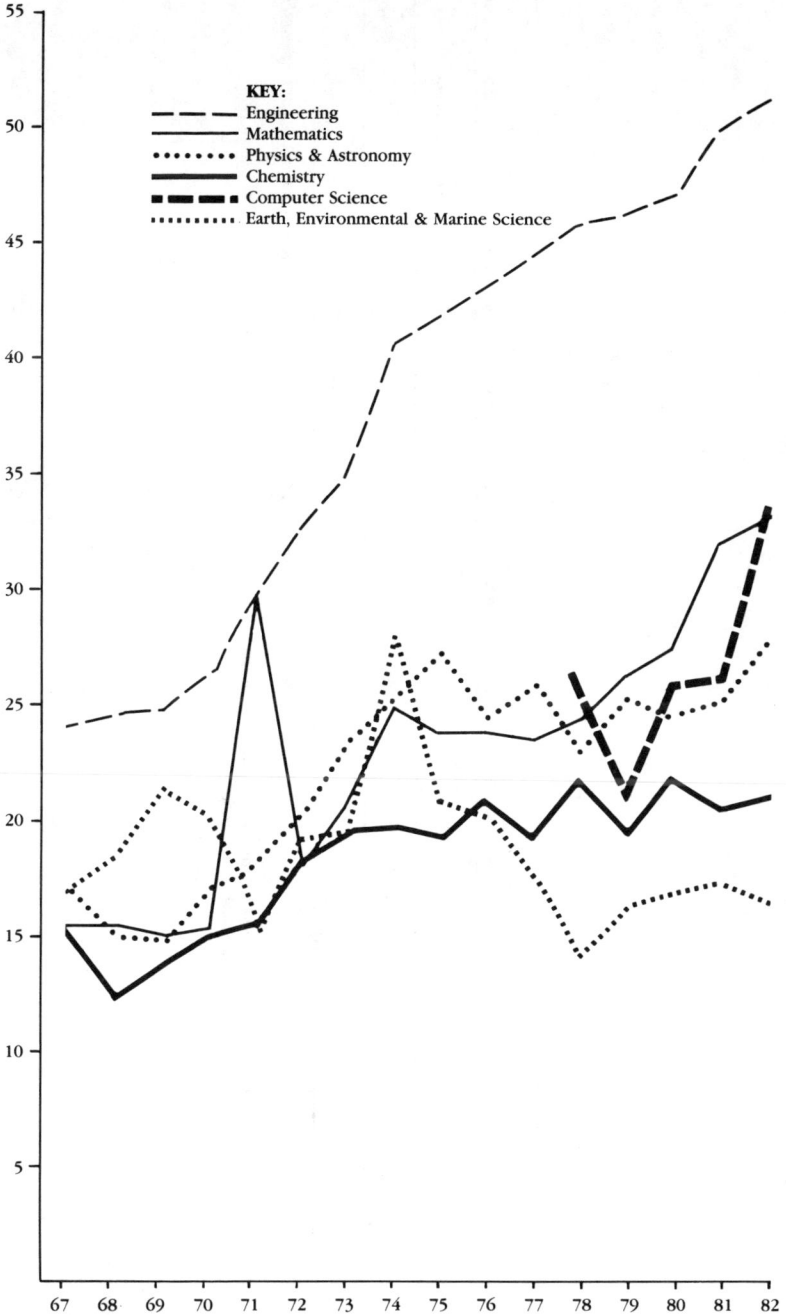

Figure 4
NATURAL SCIENCES
Percent of Doctorates Awarded to Foreign Citizens

KEY:
— — — Engineering
——— Mathematics
•••••• Physics & Astronomy
▬▬▬ Chemistry
■■■ Computer Science
••••••• Earth, Environmental & Marine Science

TABLE 12

Degrees Awarded by Level, Citizenship, and Science/Non-Science: 1980/81

	Bachelor's				Master's				Doctoral			
	Foreign Students		U.S. Students		Foreign Students		U.S. Students		Foreign Students		U.S. Students	
	Science	Non-Science	Science	Non-Science	Science	Non-Science	Science	Non-Science	Science	Non-Science	Science	Non-Science
Number	12,300	10,331	314,131	610,115	9,364	12,694	59,967	214,773	2,574	1,630	13,049	15,729
Percent	54.4	45.6	34.0	66.0	42.5	57.5	21.8	78.2	61.2	38.8	45.3	54.7

Science = *Agriculture, architecture, biological science, computer science, engineering, health science, home economics, math, military science, physical science, and psychology.*

Non-Science = *Area studies, business and management, communications, education, fine arts, foreign language, law, letters, library science, public affairs, social science, theology, interdisciplinary studies.*

Source: Higher Education General Information Survey, National Center for Educational Statistics, 1980/81

Ph.D.s is almost nil at 2 percent, with only agriculture, education, and the humanities projecting more Ph.D.s in 1988/89 than in 1980/81.

It is also interesting to note that if we use the ACE prediction of total foreign enrollments in 1988/89, the implication is that enrollment could grow by 162 percent between 1980 and 1988. Even allowing for lags between university entry and receipt of the degree, that number is quite incompatible with the projected growth in degrees awarded to foreigners of 37 percent. However, the forecast by Frances of about 60 percent growth in foreign student enrollments seems to be in line with the growth in degrees, given the lags.

Analysis of 1980/81 Degree Recipients: Costs and Subsidies

For the 1980/81 academic year, we have been able to look at earned degrees conferred for foreign and domestic students according to a variety of characteristics of the institutions awarding the degrees. This unique data base enables us to see whether foreign students are overrepresented in certain types of institutions, and so to test some of the beliefs about foreign students.

The data from NCES are provided by institution and major field of degree. For each field/institution cell, the percentage of the total number of each degree made up of foreign bachelor's, master's and doctorates was calculated. Since there are 24 fields, each institution had up to 72 percentages calculated, depending upon in how many fields each degree was awarded. Institutions were then sorted by characteristics of interest to us, and averages of the percentage of degrees that were foreign were calculated. Thus, within a cell (e.g., private institutions, bachelor's degrees, social science majors), each institution is given equal weight. To the extent that within a cell institutions of vastly different sizes have grossly different percentages of foreign students, the shares calculated are biased toward the smaller institutions, because all institutions are given equal weight regardless of their size. The tables indicate the average percentage of foreign degrees in a field by institution, *not* the number of foreign students receiving each degree divided by all students in the relevant institutions and fields.

Before reviewing tables of the type just described, we shall look at the actual number of degrees awarded in 1980/81, shown in **Table 12**. Degrees awarded are broken down according to whether students, both foreign and domestic, have studied science or "non-science."[5] Of course our division between these two broad areas could be adjusted according to other people's tastes; our categorization puts all fields with relatively high capital costs in the science group. Nevertheless, it is apparent that in our terms, at all degree levels, *foreign students are more inclined to opt for science degrees than are domestic students.* At the bachelor's level, 54.4 percent of foreign students received their degrees in science, compared to 34.0 percent of domestic students; at the master's level, 42.5 percent of foreign students and 21.8 percent of domestic students were in science; and at the doctorate level, the figures were 61.2 percent for foreign students and 45.3 percent for domestic ones.

By this measure, as well as by earlier ones using enrollment data, it is clear that the typical foreign student is in the United States to study in an area of science rather than in a "softer" field. This would imply that on average, he or she is getting relatively more expensive education than the typical American student is. In order to understand cost issues, we now turn to the NCES data on earned degrees by institution for 1980/81.

Table 13 looks at the average percentage of degrees awarded to foreigners by institutions grouped by total expenditures of all types per student. At the bachelor's level, no systematic patterns for foreign students are apparent. A slightly greater share of bachelor's degrees were awarded to foreign students at the institutions with the very highest and very lowest spending levels. However, these two extreme categories represent only 10 percent of the reporting departments (institution/field cells). Between these categories, for 90 percent of the departments, virtually no unusual concentration of foreign students was identified. On the other hand, it does appear that at the graduate level, foreign students were more likely to obtain degrees at institutions which spent more per student. For example, in the 568 departments spending less than $2,000 per student, 7.64 percent of the master's degrees were awarded to foreign students on average, whereas in the 579 departments spending more than $10,000 per student, 12.08 percent of the master's degrees were awarded to foreign students on average. Similarly, in the 253 departments which spent less than $2,000 per student, on average 6.88 percent of the Ph.D.s went to foreign students, whereas at the 409 departments spending more than $10,000, on average 14.09 percent of the doctorates went to foreigners.

Where education is more costly, that is, at the graduate level, foreign students appear likely to concentrate at relatively higher spending institutions. One reason for this is that foreign students are more likely to study science-oriented fields; and in institutions emphasizing science, education is more costly. Average costs per student are higher in institutions with graduate programs than in institutions offering only undergraduate degrees. Another reason why foreign graduate students are more likely than foreign undergraduates to enroll in relatively high-cost institutions is that quality is more likely to be an important factor in selection of institution for graduate students than for undergraduates. Quality of graduate programs is more broadly known than are quality rankings of undergraduate departments, and quality usually costs money.

If education of foreigners, particularly at the graduate level, is likely to be at institutions which spend more per student, the question arises as to whether foreign students are being subsidized when they study in this country. To shed some light on this question, each institution was categorized according to the

TABLE 13

Percentage of All Students Classified Foreign
by Total Expenditures of Institutions Attended: 1980/1981

	Bachelor's		Master's		Doctoral	
	Cells	Percent Degrees to Foreigners	Cells	Percent Degrees to Foreigners	Cells	Percent Degrees to Foreigners
Less than $2,000	799	3.58	568	7.64	253	6.88
$2,000 - $2,499	444	2.87	179	7.08	4	33.33
$2,500 - $2,999	1,174	3.28	455	6.66	37	11.61
$3,000 - $3,499	1.459	1.93	501	5.18	67	4.75
$3,500 - $3,999	2,012	2.64	801	6.72	124	10.66
$4,000 - $4,499	1,833	2.70	673	8.66	135	16.94
$4,500 - $4,999	1,905	2.20	526	6.73	131	10.31
$5,000 - $5,999	2,838	2.79	844	7.99	241	12.32
$6,000 - $6,999	1,997	2.20	635	11.05	323	15.88
$7,000 - $7,999	1,103	2.87	434	8.63	223	13.66
$8,000 - $9,999	909	2.63	402	10.07	231	12.22
$10,000 and Over	936	3.68	579	12.08	409	14.09

Sources: The Cooperative Institutional Research Program (CIRP) of UCLA and the American Council of Education and NCES, Higher Education General Information Survey, 1980-81.

average subsidy it provided to its students. The subsidy is calculated as average instructional expenditures per student plus average amount of aid awarded per student less tuition and fees charged to students. When tuition was different for in-state and out-of-state students, the out-of-state figure was used because that is what would be paid by foreign students. To the extent that foreign students do not receive aid from the institution, institutions would be less likely to be subsidizing foreign students, and so fewer foreign students would fall into the "subsidized" category.

Table 14 shows the average percentages of degrees awarded to foreign students in 21 fields overall, and the average share of each of the degrees awarded to

TABLE 14

Percentage of All Students Classified Foreign by Net Subsidy at Institutions Attended: 1980/81

	Bachelor's			Master's			Doctoral		
		Positive Subsidy			Positive Subsidy			Positive Subsidy	
	Overall % FS	0-299 % FS	300+ % FS	Overall % FS	0-299 % FS	300+ % FS	Overall % FS	0-299 % FS	300+ % FS
All Fields	2.64	2.90	4.17	8.34	8.91	9.50	13.25	12.26	13.29
Agriculture	4.79	3.41	8.73	16.95	14.78	19.18	26.43	40.12	18.65
Architecture	5.83	6.18	7.19	16.40	8.10	16.54	—	—	—
Area Studies	2.08	0.67	4.14	14.32	12.47	21.42	—	—	—
Biological Science	2.82	4.31	4.73	6.34	5.19	4.42	8.48	8.20	7.86
Business & Mgt.	3.18	2.06	5.12	9.79	12.85	12.74	17.62	13.65	8.14
Communications	1.08	0.65	2.61	7.00	2.50	9.81	—	—	—
Computer Science	5.21	5.75	8.41	22.13	26.59	31.16	20.02	15.47	18.33
Education	0.86	0.54	1.23	2.61	2.28	2.30	5.97	6.04	5.55
Engineering	10.22	10.77	15.57	28.51	44.97	28.39	35.55	31.72	41.93

Fine Arts	1.64	1.13	1.98	4.24	1.68	3.92	6.17	4.63	8.33
Foreign Languages	2.92	5.62	6.30	8.90	11.63	9.91	10.78	20.86	9.54
Health	1.37	0.84	1.53	3.95	4.90	5.27	7.90	4.44	6.22
Home Economics	1.75	3.23	2.35	5.69	3.85	7.23	—	—	—
Letters	1.65	0.73	3.39	4.86	4.08	4.98	7.65	8.32	12.69
Mathematics	4.75	7.04	4.36	12.87	15.25	15.27	19.67	19.59	12.74
Physical Science	4.60	5.28	8.70	13.72	13.45	16.80	19.76	19.61	21.85
Psychology	1.29	1.02	1.42	3.36	4.71	2.51	2.80	1.49	0.36
Public Affairs	1.31	0.87	1.55	3.16	2.21	6.19	—	—	—
Social Science	2.40	2.13	3.86	8.42	7.44	7.48	10.72	10.18	15.59
Theology	1.41	0	1.50	—	—	—	—	—	—
Interdisciplinary	1.00	1.23	2.58	5.95	3.26	2.45	—	—	—

Sources: The Cooperative Institutional Research Program (CIRP) of UCLA and the American Council of Education and NCES, Higher Education General Information Survey, 1980/81

foreign students in institutions where the subsidy is positive, that is, where students pay less than what their education (plus aid) costs the institution. It does appear that *at the bachelor's level, in virtually all fields, on average a higher percentage of degrees are awarded to foreign students by departments in institutions where the subsidy is positive and greater than $300 than are awarded to foreign students overall.* Although foreign students seem relatively evenly distributed among institutions which spend different amounts, they seem more likely to focus on institutions which charge them less than cost, whatever that cost is.

At the graduate level, foreign students receiving degrees are also usually disproportionately represented at institutions where they are subsidized, but, as **Table 14** showed, there are more fields in which the average proportion of degrees awarded to foreigners is smaller at institutions where students are subsidized than at all institutions combined. At the graduate level, foreign students do tend to concentrate somewhat in institutions which spend more per student, but, probably due to the higher tuition they pay, they are less likely to pay less than the cost of their education.

These findings, although perhaps paradoxical at first glance, are understandable. Particularly at the undergraduate level, foreign students come to the United States for a variety of reasons. Certainly, quality of the educational experience is an important factor. But, as is the case for American students, going to college involves choices about location, ambiance, extracurricular activities, and so on. For foreign students, desires to avoid political problems at home and ability to adapt can be added to the list of reasons for choosing a college abroad. To the extent that institutional expenditures per student reflect quality of education, we should expect that to be only one of many factors determining choice of institution by foreign undergraduate students.

On the other hand, given the variety of motives for such a choice, the probability that foreign undergraduates come to the United States with large amounts of nonfamily financial support (i.e., from the government, international agencies, or employers) is low. Thus, finding a school where the cost burden is low can be a prime concern to the foreign undergraduate. The unsystematic distribution of foreign undergraduates by institutional expenditures per student, along with a concentration where subsidy is greatest, makes sense.

At the graduate level, we would expect more foreign students to come to the United States already subsidized. The knowledge and degrees foreign graduate students acquire are surely perceived to have great social value back home. Employers, governments, and international agencies concerned with economic development in the Third World, or with improved international understanding, are likely to put their resources behind graduate rather than undergraduate students. Even though graduate students are more likely to select more expensive institutions than are undergraduates (because educational quality is more con-

TABLE 15
Number of Foreign Students Receiving Degrees
by Level of Institutional Subsidy: 1980/81

	Bachelor's	Master's	Doctoral
− $3,350 or Less	2,192	3,257	524
− $3,349 to − $2,600	1,570	2,306	282
− $2,599 to − $2,150	1,563	1,850	329
− $2,149 to − $1,750	1,829	1,454	289
− $1,749 to − $1,350	2,343	2,359	558
− $1,349 to − $950	2,276	2,394	438
− $949 to − $550	1,846	981	166
− $549 to − $200	1,777	1,642	485
− $199 to 0	1,143	686	43
$1 to $299	1,738	1,485	346
$300 or More	3,591	2,481	512
Percent Receiving Subsidy	23.5	18.0	20.4

Sources: The Cooperative Institutional Research Program (CIRP) of UCLA and the American Council of
Education and NCES, Higher Education General Information Survey, 1980/81

sistent with the goals of graduate students than with those of undergraduates),
they are likely to be able to cover the costs of their education. Thus, the finding
that foreign graduates are disproportionately at high-spending institutions and
are less likely than are undergraduates to seek institutions with subsidies seems
consistent with the reasons for institutional choice and the rationale for support
of students from abroad.

Table 15 enables us to look at actual numbers of foreign degree recipients
who graduated from institutions with different subsidy levels.[6] The most striking
finding from this table is the small share of foreign degree recipients at all degree
levels who actually pay less than the cost of their education. At the bachelor's
level, 23.5 percent of foreign degree recipients (5,329 people) attended institutions at which the subsidy was positive; at the master's level, 18.0 percent (3,966

people) received degrees where the subsidy was positive; and 20.4 percent (858 people) of foreign doctorate recipients were subsidized in this sense.

This may be a surprising finding to some people. One negative assertion about foreign students often has been that they are using funds of domestic taxpayers. The "contributory principle" of government expenditure states, "Thou shalt not enjoy the services rendered by government if thou or thy parents have contributed not to the public exchequer!" (Blaug, 1981). Then, if foreign students are subsidized, the only justification for doing so would be if benefits of having foreign students exceeded other costs of having them by more than the subsidy.

The isolated situations of certain foreign students not being able to meet financial obligations, which derive from exchange rate problems, balance of payments problems, or other economic or political crises, have been given much publicity.. And much of the data on subsidies to foreign students come from countries like Britain, where, before a special fee increment for foreign students was implemented, costs to all students were much below the costs of providing the education they received.

The situation in the United States is quite different from the case of Britain and countries like it. High out-of-state tuitions, along with large student bodies (enabling economies of scale), and little aid to foreign students in many fields, makes plausible the finding that foreigners usually pay their way.

If foreign graduates receive less financial aid from their American institutions than domestic students do, the share of them who are subsidized is even smaller than reported. On the other hand, the concentration of foreign students in "expensive" fields like science and engineering probably means that overall institutional average costs and subsidy figures overstate the share of costs that foreign students pay themselves. We must also remember that support services for foreign students are an additional cost to the universities. At minimum, it is clear that most foreign students graduate from institutions where the typical out-of-state or foreign student pays the full cost of his or her education.

By assuming that foreign students either received a subsidy or paid costs of the amounts indicated by the mid-points of the ranges of subsidies listed on the left-hand side of **Table 15,** we determined that overall, as much as $62,900,000 might be being contributed by foreign students in their final year of schooling in the United States. This averages out to $1,346 per graduate. If we assume that undergraduates are subsidized or pay only half as much as graduate students, and that costs of education for foreign students are double the costs of educating domestic students, the net contribution by foreign graduates to American institutions of higher education falls to $25,133,000, or $538 per graduate. If all 286,000 foreign students on average contributed only half that amount per student, it is possible that foreign students, on balance, added over $75 million to the net revenues of American institutions of higher education in 1980.

TABLE 16

Percentage of All Students Who Are Foreign:
Averages by Institution and by Degree Level: 1980/81

Institution Control

		Bachelor's	Master's	Doctoral
Public	Number	6,876	3,982	1,253
	Percent	2.55	8.37	14.05
Private	Number	9,945	2,122	678
	Percent	2.72	8.25	11.75

Type of Institution

		Bachelor's	Master's	Doctorate
University	Number	2,637	2,425	1,558
	Percent	2.68	10.46	13.34
Four-Year	Number	14,182	3,679	373
	Percent	2.64	6.92	12.84

Sources: The Cooperative Institutional Research Program (CIRP) of UCLA and the American Council of Education and NCES, Higher Education General Information Survey, 1980/81

These numbers are only speculative at this point. More analysis should and could be done with available data. However, it is suggested here that foreign students probably pay more than their education costs, and they might be paying substantially more.

Other Characteristics of 1980/81 Degree Recipients

The analysis of degree recipients from the NCES data enables us to look at several factors involved in choice of institution by foreign students.

Table 16 looks at the types of institutions chosen by foreign students who are graduating relative to those chosen by all students who are graduating. At the bachelor's level, foreign students are slightly overrepresented in private institutions but are equally proportional to all students at universities and four-year colleges. At the graduate level (both master's and doctorate), foreign students represent slightly larger shares in public institutions and, as would be expected, in universities.

Table 13 revealed a disproportionately high share of foreign students graduating with masters or Ph.D.s in high-cost institutions; yet **Table 14** showed graduate students in many fields to be paying more than their education costs. It seems then that foreigners are graduating with masters and doctorates from either high-cost public or private institutions, but are selecting those institutions of both types which charge (out-of-state) tuition which is high enough to cover instructional costs.

Table 17 shows that foreign undergraduate students are overrepresented at the low-selectivity institutions, whereas graduate students concentrate relatively more at medium- to high-selectivity schools. This confirms the hypothesis that quality may be less important at the baccalaureate level. Also, even though many top graduate programs encourage foreign enrollments, weaker programs seem more willing to allow foreigners to comprise a greater share of their classes, particularly at the doctoral level.

TABLE 17
Percentage of All Students Who Are Foreign:
Averages by Degree Level and Quality of Institution Selected: 1980/81

| | Bachelor's | | Master's | | Doctoral | |
	Percent	Number	Percent	Number	Percent	Number
Low	3.16	8,391	8.08	2,672	11.57	634
Medium	2.00	3,725	8.20	1,457	14.52	580
High	2.24	2,917	10.47	1,199	13.67	664

Sources: The Cooperative Institutional Research Program (CIRP) of UCLA and the American Council of Education and NCES, Higher Education General Information Survey, 1980/81

Table 18 attempted to see if foreign students were overrepresented in large urban areas. The idea here was that foreign students tend to select programs located in cities which are well known abroad, certainly not a highly relevant educational motive. This hypothesis seems to be confirmed at the bachelor's level; 4.65 percent of baccalaureate recipients were in institutions in cities of greater than two million, with the next highest share of foreign graduates being 2.97 percent in suburban areas surrounding cities of over two million people. This trend toward large metropolitan areas is also revealed by master's recipients, although more weakly so. At the doctoral level, the distribution of foreign graduates by city size is virtually flat, implying that this is a relatively insignificant factor in choice of department. Since the quality of doctoral programs should be of greater concern than should be quality at other degree levels, this finding is reasonable.

Our preliminary analysis of 1980/81 foreign graduates seems to imply that undergraduates are more concerned with out-of-pocket costs, and less concerned with quality than are graduate students. Given the wider range of motives of foreign undergraduates for attending U.S. colleges, and given the greater likelihood that graduate students will be subsidized from sources other than family

TABLE 18

Percentage of All Students Who Are Foreign:
Averages by Degree Level and City Size: 1980/81

	Bachelor's		Master's		Doctoral	
	Number	Percent	Number	Percent	Number	Percent
Outside SMSA	5,549	2.23	1,561	8.32	371	15.10
Less than 250,000	2,252	2.07	760	7.15	256	12.02
250,000–499,999	1,988	2.72	790	9.27	247	14.45
500,000–999,999	2,176	2.40	870	6.34	250	11.49
Suburban 1 Million	407	1.68	150	7.89	65	16.58
Urban 1 Million	1,011	2.79	454	8.46	164	12.10
Suburban 2 Million	1,639	2.97	567	7.95	163	15.79
Urban 2 Million	1,744	4.65	942	10.33	415	11.62

Sources: The Cooperative Institutional Research Program (CIRP) of UCLA and the American Council of Education and NCES, Higher Education General Information Survey, 1980/81

or the receiving institution, these findings make a great deal of intuitive sense.

Slippery Cost/Benefit Analysis

In reviewing the literature concerning the impact of the foreign student on the American university and community, several recurring arguments can be discerned. These range from those which advocate positive cultural and educational benefits to those which stress more negative economic and technological issues. It is rare, however, that a full and systematic examination of these arguments is undertaken. This is the aim of the present section of the paper. Even though we are unable to identify costs and benefits with certainty, and though we cannot put a dollar value on any of them, the reader can decide which arguments are most likely, and hence, whether there are net costs or net benefits to welcoming foreign students. The difficulty of this task explains why we have described our analysis as "slippery."

FOOTNOTES

1. Even if the rate of growth is not as predicted by ACE, the work of Carol Francis cited below is probably close to the mark. Her anticipated growth rate to 1990 is about 500,000. Nevertheless, we begin with the larger growth estimate to point out how large some knowledgeable people believe the foreign student population could soon become.

2. Frances (1980) has taken a less optimistic view and hypothesized that "with the growing prosperity of the less developed nations, and the pressure for an increasing rate of transfer of industrial technology, we might anticipate a continuing increase in the number of foreign students in the United States in the 1980s. . . ." If the number doubled from 1980 to 1990, the total enrollment could increase by 280,000 students. That would lead to 560,000 foreign students by 1990, compared to the 804,000 predicted by ACE (1982). Thus the forecast discussed in the text requires even greater optimism that most people are willing to accept.

3. Although humanities and fine arts are combined in **Table 1,** we separated these two groups of fields for purposes of the present discussion.

4. Moreover, on February 17, 1984, the National Science Foundation issued a report which said shortages scientists and engineers in industry were down substantially from 1982 to 1983. Thus, the problem of foreign students taking classroom places away from American engineering prospects may become less of a problem very soon. If industrial demand falls, the relative compensation offered by academe should improve, thus increasing the incentive for highly trained engineers to take academic jobs.

5. Science degrees are in the fields of agriculture, architecture, biological science, computer science, engineering, health science, home economics, mathematics, military science, physical science, and psychology. Non-science includes area studies, business and management, communications, education, fine arts, foreign languages, law, letters, library science, public affairs, social science, theology, and interdisciplinary studies.

6. At least 94 percent of the foreign degree recipients were able to be classified by level of institutional subsidy.

Editor's Note

This book is the result of a conference held at the Spring Hill Center in Wayzata, Minnesota, from April 13-15, 1984. The conference was organized by the Institute of International Education and supported by grants from the Exxon Education Foundation, the General Service Foundation, and a subsidy from the Spring Hill Center.

The high quality of the book reflects both the contributions made by the authors of the two background papers to the conceptualization of the sources and impacts of foreign student flows and the skill of the participants in the conference in assessing the meaning of these flows, particularly from the point of view of different types of institutions of higher education. The quality of the conference itself benefited from the excellent services of the Spring Hill Center; the director of Spring Hill, James Kelley, made valuable suggestions of possible participants in the conference to IIE staff.

IIE is grateful for all the different contributions that made the Spring Hill conference and the resulting book possible.

List of Attendants

Steve Altman
Vice-President, Academic Affairs
Florida International University

Elinor G. Barber
Director of Research
Institute of International Education

Ed Battle
Director of Communications
Institute of International Education

Lorna Blake
Director of Admissions
Smith College

Carmen Brown
Director of Admissions
Florida International University

Alice Chandler
President
State University of New York College
    at New Paltz

Peter de Villiers
Department of Psychology
Smith College

Theodore Galambos
Department of Civil and Mineral
    Engineering
University of Minnesota

Craufurd Goodwin
Office of the Vice-Provost
Duke University

Patricia Hansen
Vice-President, Student Affairs
Florida International University

Stephen Hoenack
Office of the President
University of Minnesota

Stephen Horn
President
California State University

Alex Inkeles
Hoover Institution

Sanford Jameson
College Entrance Examination Board

Robert Kaplan
President
National Association of Foreign
    Student Affairs

Margaret A. Kidd
International Office
University of Texas

Reatha Clark King
President
Metropolitan State University

K. William Leffland
International Affairs Center
Florida International University

Larry Litten
Consortium on Financing of Higher
Education

Seamus Malin
Admissions Office
Harvard University

Michael Nacht
Kennedy School of Government
Harvard University

Joe Neal
Director, International Office
University of Texas

William Paver
Admissions Office
University of Texas

Cassandra Pyle
Division of International Education
American Council on Education

John E. Reichard
National Association of Foreign
Student Affairs

Piedad F. Robertson
Vice-President for Public Affairs
Miami-Dade Community College

Larry Sirowy
Hoover Institution

David Smock
Vice-President, Development and
Research
Institute of International Education

Lewis Solmon
Graduate School of Education
University of California at Los Angeles

Charles Sorber
Associate Dean, Engineering School
University of Texas

Manfred Stassen
German Academic Exchange Service

Kenneth W. Tolo
Associate Vice-President, Academic
Affairs
University of Texas

John Wallace
Assistant Vice-President, Academic
Affairs
University of Minnesota

Wendy Winters
Office of the Dean of the College
Smith College

Gregory B. Wolfe
President
Florida International University

John Eng Wong
Brown University